SUBDIVISION ANALYSIS

Readers of this text may be interested in the following related texts: *The Appraisal of Real Estate*, tenth edition; *The Dictionary of Real Estate Appraisal*, third edition; and *Hotels and Motels: A Guide to Market Analysis, Investment Analysis, and Valuations.*

For a catalog of Appraisal Institute publications, contact the PR/Marketing Department of the Appraisal Institute, 875 North Michigan Avenue, Chicago, Illinois 60611-1980.

SUBDIVISION ANALYSIS

Douglas D. Lovell, MAI
Robert S. Martin, MAI, SRA

**APPRAISAL
INSTITUTE**

Appraisal Institute
875 N. Michigan Avenue
Chicago, Illinois 60611-1980

Acknowledgments

Reviewers: Thomas A. Motta, MAI, SRA
James H. Bulthuis, MAI, SRA
Gary P. Taylor, MAI, SRA

Vice President, Publications: Christopher Bettin
Manager, Book Development: Michael R. Milgrim, PhD
Editor: Stephanie Shea-Joyce
Manager, Design/Production: Julie Beich

For Educational Purposes Only

The opinions and statements set forth herein reflect the viewpoint of the Appraisal Institute at the time of publication but do not necessarily reflect the viewpoint of each individual member. While a great deal of care has been taken to provide accurate and current information, neither the Appraisal Institute nor its editors and staff assume responsibility for the accuracy of the data contained herein. Further, the general principles and conclusions presented in this text are subject to local, state and federal laws and regulations, court cases and any revisions of the same. This publication is sold for educational purposes with the understanding that the publisher is not engaged in rendering legal, accounting or any other professional service.

Nondiscrimination Policy

The Appraisal Institute advocates equal opportunity and nondiscrimination in the appraisal profession and conducts its activities without regard to race, color, sex, religion, national origin, or handicap status.

Printed in the United States of America
The photos appearing in this text were supplied by H. Armstrong Roberts, Inc.

Library of Congress Cataloging-in-Publication Data

Lovell, Douglas D.
Subdivision Analysis/Douglas D. Lovell, Robert S. Martin
p.   cm.
ISBN 0-922194-11-2
1. Real property—Valuation.   2. Land subdivision.   I. Martin.
Robert S.   II. Title.
HD1387.L7   1993
333.33'2—dc20

Table of Contents

▼▼▼

Foreword

Although subdivisions have been an important part of the American landscape for nearly 50 years, there is a dearth of literature on their valuation. This new monograph, *Subdivision Analysis*, addresses this need and explores the intricacies of the appraisal and analysis of subdivision developments.

All the key elements of subdivision valuation are covered—the identification of highest and best use, the analysis of project feasibility and marketability, financial modeling techniques, the evaluation of project risk, and the applicability of each of the three approaches to value.

Readers are instructed in the estimation of both raw land value and the prospective value of the entire subdivision property upon completion. A detailed case study is presented to demonstrate how the subdivision analysis method is applied and how it can be modified so that the timing of cash receipts and disbursements matches the anticipated cash flow pattern of the specific property.

This long-awaited text provides a wealth of practical information, illuminating a complicated and often perplexing area of real estate appraisal.

Bernard J. Fountain, MAI, SRA
1993 President
Appraisal Institute

▼▼▼

About the Authors

Douglas D. Lovell, MAI, has broad experience in the private and public sectors as an appraiser, loan workout specialist, and educator. He has prepared and presented educational programs on commercial real estate loan underwriting, financial analysis of savings and loan institutions, loan management, appraisal policies, real estate decision-making strategy, and the requirements of the Federal Home Loan Bank Board. His articles have appeared in a variety of real estate and financial publications. Lovell has a BSBA degree from the University of Florida and an MBA from the University of Central Florida.

Robert S. Martin, MAI, SRA, CRE, is a real estate appraiser in Winston-Salem, North Carolina. Educated at Duke University and the Emory University Graduate School of Business Administration, Martin is the developer of the Appraisal Institute's Advanced Applications course and several seminars on a variety real estate appraisal subjects.

▼▼▼

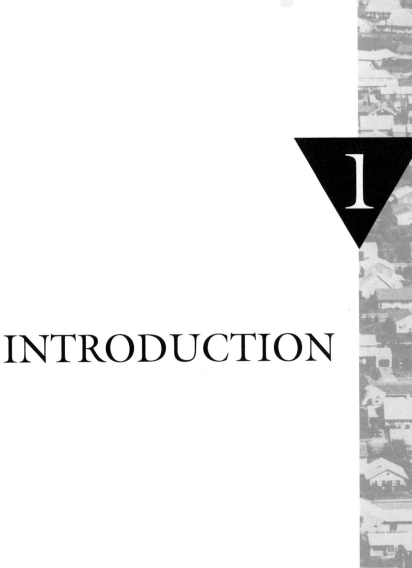

INTRODUCTION

PURPOSE OF THE MONOGRAPH

The valuation of subdivided real estate has long been recognized as one of the most challenging types of assignments confronting appraisers. The proper handling of such assignments requires a comprehensive knowledge of market analysis and forecasting techniques. A thorough understanding of financial modeling is also needed to produce logical, supportable estimates of value.

Although subdivision analysis is an important part of modern appraisal practice, relatively little literature is available on the subject. This problem was recognized in 1973 when the National Appraisal Review Committee and the Education Committee of the American Institute of Real Estate

Appraisers issued *Educational Memorandum No. 1 Subdivision Analysis*. This important work introduced acceptable procedures for the valuation of subdivision acreage.[1]

As time passed it became evident that a more definitive treatment of subdivision analysis was needed. In response to this need, the American Institute of Real Estate Appraisers revised the original subdivision memorandum and reissued it in 1978 under the title *Subdivision Analysis*. This second publication included much more information than the earlier memorandum and provided clear guidelines concerning unacceptable practices. Moreover, each method described in the revised memorandum was followed by a discussion of its advantages and disadvantages.[2]

Both of these publications were important contributions to appraisal literature, but their scope was limited to the valuation of raw land. Extending the basic concept to cover other valuation problems was left to others. Over the past 20 years a handful of authors have made important new contributions to subdivision analysis technique. Unfortunately, their efforts have not been directed systematically; some important issues have been covered in several publications, while others have not been addressed at all. This information gap has been most evident in the analysis of proposed subdivision properties, where appraisers must estimate the value of the project as a whole upon completion.

This monograph will address many issues that have not received sufficient attention in the past and explore techniques brought about by the evolution of appraisal methodology over the past two decades.

OBJECTIVES OF SUBDIVISION ANALYSIS

The traditional objective of subdivision analysis is the valuation of raw land. When properly applied, the subdivision method produces reliable value

---

1. American Institute of Real Estate Appraisers, *Educational Memorandum No. 1 Subdivision Analysis* (Chicago: American Institute of Real Estate Appraisers, 1973), 3–5.

2. American Institute of Real Estate Appraisers, *Subdivision Analysis* (Chicago: American Institute of Real Estate Appraisers, 1978), 1–20.

estimates because it simulates the decision-making processes of a typical purchaser of land suitable for development. Ideally, such estimates would be consistent with the results produced by sales comparison analysis.

Because the sophistication of real estate investors and lenders has increased, many appraisers are now called upon to estimate not only the value of the raw land, but also the prospective value of the entire subdivision property upon completion. Appraisers have found that by modifying the traditional subdivision analysis methodology they can supply their clients with additional value estimates and estimate the value of a development at various points in time or stages of completion.

APPLICATIONS OF SUBDIVISION ANALYSIS METHODOLOGY

One reason subdivision analysis has proven to be applicable to other valuation problems is its flexibility. The technique is designed to simulate the behavior of typical market participants, who are keenly interested in the timing of cash receipts and disbursements and in quantifying the risks associated with a venture. The subdivision valuation method allows the user to modify the timing of cash receipts and disbursements to match the expected cash flow pattern of the specific property. With this flexibility appraisers can estimate both the value of a raw site and the prospective value of the property once it is completed.

A further advantage of this methodology is that it allows the appraiser to arrive at a logical conclusion even when comparable market data are lacking. For example, sales data are rarely available to estimate the value of a partially completed subdivision property. When correctly applied, the financial modeling techniques employed in the subdivision analysis method provide the appraiser with a means to answer logically the question of how much a partially completed subdivision might be worth.

▼▼▼

RELATIONSHIP TO OTHER VALUATION TECHNIQUES

To understand how subdivision analysis relates to other valuation techniques, it is important to remember that subdivision analysis represents only one approach to value. Both cost and sales comparison techniques are applicable to subdivision properties and should be used as they would be in other types of valuation assignments. The subdivision method is essentially an income approach which measures the financial rewards, risks, and costs associated with a real estate investment.

Perhaps the most important benefit of including the cost and sales comparison approaches in a subdivision appraisal is that they can serve as a cross-check on the validity of the subdivision methodology. If, for example, current market sales do not support the value of a subdivision site derived by the subdivision method, the method should be reevaluated. Inconsistencies between valuation methods may indicate forecasting errors or improper application.

A lack of comparable sales is often cited as a reason for excluding the sales comparison approach. However, the lack of sales data does not reflect the marketability and investment risks associated with subdivision properties. Rather, it is generally due to the fact that completed subdivisions may not typically be sold in a specific market area upon completion, but over a period prior to sellout.

The cost approach is also important in subdivision valuation. If the total cost of a development exceeds its value at completion, the venture may not be economically feasible.

In many instances the exclusion of other approaches to value seriously weakens an appraiser's analysis.

THE VALUATION PROCESS

Identification of the Appraisal Problem

The valuation process is a systematic procedure that provides the answer to a client's question about real property value. Although the steps followed in

▼▼▼

the valuation process may vary with the nature of the appraisal assignment, the basic pattern of problem identification, market research, data analysis, application of valuation techniques, reconciliation of value indications, and final value conclusion can be applied to any appraisal assignment.[3]

The valuation process begins with identification of the appraisal problem. Problem identification is important because the nature of the decision facing the client will determine the character of the assignment and the subsequent report. To avoid wasted effort, the appraiser and the client should discuss the use of the appraisal report and its conclusions.

Use of the Appraisal Report

A subdivision appraisal may be used for a variety of purposes. For example, a value estimate may be needed to

- Estimate the market value of a property
- Set a purchase or selling price
- Establish the amount of a loan
- Determine the basis for taxation
- Estimate just compensation in eminent domain proceedings

Because the use of the appraisal will greatly affect the depth of the analysis undertaken and the content of the report prepared, the appraiser must understand the use of the report. Appraisals that do not properly address the client's needs will invariably be viewed as inappropriate by the client; a report can be very misleading if the appraiser has not properly identified the appraisal problem.

Land Valuation

Most land valuation assignments involve estimating the worth of the site "as is." The "as is" value should reflect the worth of the property as it physically and legally exists on the date of valuation. Assumptions regarding a

---

3. Appraisal Institute, *The Appraisal of Real Estate*, 10th ed. (Chicago: Appraisal Institute, 1992), 71–82.

change in the legally permitted use of the property should be avoided, unless they can be demonstrated to be reasonable. If changes in use would not be anticipated by typical purchasers, the appraiser should avoid making unfounded assertions as to the impact a proposed change might have on the value of the property.

Assignments involving proposed projects may call for an estimate of property value as of the anticipated date of completion (prospective value).

Completed projects Many valuation assignments involving proposed projects require an appraiser to estimate the value of the property at the point in time when the property is expected to be completed. Under such an assumption, the value estimate produced is a prospective estimate rather than a current estimate. Since value is time dependent, the appraiser should state the specific date when completion is forecast to occur as well as the date the appraisal was prepared.[4]

Sometimes an appraiser is asked to prepare a value estimate assuming that the property is complete on the date the appraisal is prepared. Caution should be exercised in such assignments because hypothetical value estimates can be misleading and inappropriate if the value is not properly identified. Hypothetical valuations should generally be avoided unless there is strong market support for the client's assumption.

Multiphase projects Multiphase projects[5] pose special valuation problems, especially when the development plan calls for the installation of infrastruc-

---

4. See Standards Rule 2-2(e) of the Uniform Standards of Professional Appraisal Practice.
5. See Chapter 5 for a description of multiphase projects.

▼▼▼

▼▼

ture that will service more than one project phase. To assess the contributory value of the infrastructure in such a case, the appraiser must first estimate the economic viability of the overall development plan. This may be extremely difficult because final plans and specifications for all planned phases are often not available.

Economic viability cannot be assumed. If adequate plans for the entire project are not available, the appraiser must determine the feasibility of the phases for which plans have been developed. To evaluate the economic viability of a project, it may be necessary to include the cost of the total infrastructure in the cost of the initial project phases for which plans are available.

When complete plans and specifications for a multiphase project are available, the appraiser may need to produce multiple value estimates. Separate estimates may be needed to reflect the value of each development phase upon completion and the value of any remaining land.

Partially completed projects

Most assignments involving partially completed developments require an appraiser to estimate both the current "as is" value of the property and its prospective value upon completion. In such situations the "as is" value estimate should reflect the worth of the property on the date the value is estimated. If the "as is" value estimate assumes eventual completion of the development, the appraiser should state this fact and include the reasoning on which this assumption is based.

For partially completed projects, both an "as is" value and a prospective value estimate may be required.

In appraising a partially completed development, the appraiser should clearly explain why the project has not been completed. If the project failed for any reason, the appraiser should assess its prospects for future success. The analysis should carefully consider the effect of any stigma associated with the project and estimate any additional costs associated with completing it. In estimating the prospective value of such properties upon completion, the appraiser should follow the same guidelines applicable to completed projects.

Identification of the Property Rights to Be Valued

Every real estate appraisal should precisely identify the property rights being valued. The reader of the report should not have to speculate as to the nature or quality of the rights associated with the property.

If the nature or quality of the property rights is not known, the services of a professional may be needed to identify all the important limitations affecting the ownership position.

Identification of the Real Estate

Identification of the real estate includes a legal description of the property being appraised as well as the point or points in time when the project's value will be estimated. The property should be identified using the method of legal description commonly required to transfer ownership interests in the jurisdiction where the property is located.

Definition of Value

It is imperative that the appraisal precisely identify the value being estimated. Market value is defined in various ways and each definition is unique. Therefore, the appraisal report must not only state the type of value being estimated, but also should contain the full text of the definition used by the appraiser.

In some assignments appraisers develop their market value estimates assuming that specific financing terms will be available to a typical purchaser. The specification of typical financing should have no impact on the final value estimate reached. The appraiser should recognize, however, that the imposition of below-market financing terms may result in an investment value estimate rather than a market value estimate. Because below-market financing assumptions can result in a higher value estimate, the Uniform Standards of Professional Appraisal Practice require that specific information relative to the impact of such assumptions be included in the appraisal report.[6]

In addition to estimating the market value of the property "as is," the appraiser may also be asked to estimate the prospective value of the project upon completion but prior to sellout of the lots. When estimating the prospective value upon completion, the estimate derived in each valuation approach applied should reflect the appraiser's best judgment as to the value of the property when the project is completed. Moreover, the appraiser must specifically identify the expected date of completion in the appraisal report.

Market value is an estimate while market price is an accomplished fact. Market value has been defined as "the price that would tend to prevail under typical (nonsubsidized) competitive open market conditions."[7] It is important to remember that an estimate of market value, regardless of its effective date, may never become an accomplished fact and thus may not be subject to verification. For example, an appraiser may estimate the market value of a vacant site at a certain sum, but the actual selling price of the land may differ significantly from the appraiser's estimate. The fact that the appraiser's estimate was not verified by actual market activity does not mean that the estimate was erroneous. The difference may be the result of changes in market conditions between the date the value was estimated and the date the property was actually sold. Alternatively, the terms and conditions of the actual sale may be very different than those assumed to prevail when the market value estimate was made. Such variations are quite common and should not be cause for concern as long as the appraiser's estimates are properly documented and supported.

---

6. See Standards Rule 1–2(b)(iii) of the Uniform Standards of Professional Appraisal Practice.

7. Byrl N. Boyce and William N. Kinnard, Jr., *Appraising Real Property* (Lexington, Mass.: Lexington Books, 1987), 7.

In deciding whether to identify a prospective value estimate as market value, the real issue is whether the analytical process applied to develop the estimate was reasonable and properly supported by market evidence. A market price does not have to be justified because it is an historic fact. A market value estimate, on the other hand, must be substantiated because it is an estimate of "what would be or should be under assumed market conditions."[8]

Assumptions and Limiting Conditions

The underlying assumptions and limiting conditions of the appraisal are an integral part of every appraisal report. In establishing the assumptions and limiting conditions that are applicable, the appraiser considers both ethical and practical concerns.

All important assumptions and limiting conditions should be clearly stated. In lengthy reports it is often useful to identify specific assumptions at the point where they are used in the analysis and to list all the assumptions in one place in the report. Many clients prefer to see assumptions listed in one section because it simplifies the review process and helps them understand the appraisal better.

Because professional practice standards have a direct bearing on what assumptions are considered permissible, appraisers should have a thorough understanding of the reporting standards and ethical rules that govern their work. A problem may arise when an appraiser is requested to provide only the hypothetical value of a proposed project as if it were completed. Such a request may not be a problem if the estimate is clearly identified as a hypothetical value and the limited scope of the assignment is specifically stated, but some clients might object to a report that contains such wording. In this case the appraiser might be tempted to remove the objectionable wording and place this information in the limiting conditions section of the report, which might result in a misleading appraisal.

Ideally, an appraisal should fairly present all evidence relevant to the solution of the valuation problem. No material information should be withheld or omitted.

---

8. Ibid.

ANALYSIS OF THE COMPONENTS OF A SUBDIVISION

KEY ELEMENTS OF A SUBDIVISION

A subdivision is much more than a group of physical components. A subdivision is composed of a variety of tangible and intangible elements which contribute to the project's ultimate value and utility.

One of the most useful ways to analyze a subdivision is in terms of its economic components: land, labor, capital, and entrepreneurial reward. Viewing a subdivision in this fashion focuses the analytic process on a productive property operation, not a fragmented assembly of unrelated parts.

▼▼▼

11

A location near natural amenities can contribute to the success of a subdivision development.

Land

Land is one of the most fundamental components of a subdivision property. In an economic sense land contributes much more than just a physical location for the development. The key contribution of the land is its relationship to the surrounding competitive market. For this reason it is often said that the three most important factors affecting the value of a property are location, location, location.

The importance of location to the success of a subdivision cannot be overstated. Real estate developments do not exist in a vacuum. They must compete with other properties and, to a great extent, a subdivision's ability to compete in the marketplace depends on its locational attributes. The proximity of a development to natural amenities such as lakes, rivers, and mountains can make the difference between a successful project and one that is only marginally successful. In urban and suburban markets, factors such as highway access, proximity to major employment markets, and access to mass transportation may combine with the natural amenities of a site to create a superior development.

One of the principal tasks involved in the valuation of a subdivision property is identification of the specific locational features that affect the property being appraised. The analytic process should focus on both the positive and negative features affecting the subject and competing developments. A simple listing of their qualitative features is insufficient. The analyst must convert the qualitative data into quantitative information so that the economic viability of the venture can be addressed.

Another major characteristic influencing the value of land is its physical attributes. Factors such as topography can affect a site both positively and negatively. For example, a hilly terrain may result in the positive benefit of a view amenity but also increase the costs to install sewer, water, and street improvements. The shape of a site relates to its overall usability. An unusual configuration can lead to an inefficient layout as well as increased development costs.

The size of the site may also influence the developer's ability to design an efficient project. The size of the development must be properly scaled to match the ability of the market to absorb the completed lots. Analysis may indicate that only a portion of the site has a current highest and best use as a subdivision, while the remaining acreage has future development potential.

Similarly, the size of the site may necessitate the installation of infrastructure for the entire project although only a portion of the development plan will be carried out immediately. If the feasibility of the overall project is not adequately addressed, the appraiser may reach erroneous conclusions about the appropriateness of the development.

Phased projects can be difficult to appraise, especially if the scale of the project is large relative to the overall market supply and the probability of success must be forecast over an extended period. In analyzing such projects forecasting errors can be difficult to quantify and compensate for, which may lead to uncertain results.

A final factor to be considered in valuing the land component of a subdivision property is the impact of soil conditions. For a subdivision development to be successful, the developed lots must be able to support the type of improvements for which they are intended. Land that lacks bearing capacity may be unsuitable for any type of development or, in less extreme cases, the cost of development may be prohibitive. If a site has rock formations just beneath its surface, extensive blasting may be required to install the underground utilities. Adverse environmental conditions due to the presence of toxic waste on a site may add significant clean-up expenses to development costs. If such costs are not properly considered in evaluating the economic feasibility of a project, the project may fail even though it originally appeared to be feasible.

Labor

In most real estate developments, land is only one factor of production that must be considered. To be used productively, land must be combined with the other factors of production.

In subdivision properties, the labor component is reflected in site improvements, development plans, marketing efforts, legal fees, and project overhead. Because the labor expended on the development is one of the most significant factors of production, it must be analyzed carefully.

Expenditures for goods and services do not automatically add to a project's value; capital must be expended in a productive fashion to contribute to the value of the project. Expenditures for unproductive components may not be recoverable and will only serve to increase development costs.

In assessing labor costs it is important to identify not only the specific expenditures that are anticipated, but also their timing. In estimating anticipated labor expenditures, the analyst should include all hard and soft costs necessary to implement the development plan. Estimates designed to reflect the costs incurred to achieve a particular point of completion should include only those expenditures needed to reach that point of completion. For example, a cost-of-completion estimate will normally not include marketing expenditures because these expenses are not incurred until after the project is completed.

The analyst must carefully study the timing of expenditures in relation to the actual product being produced. Expenditures that do not relate to the production of a salable product add to project overhead, which may not be recoverable. For example, the cost of installing infrastructure unrelated to the specific project phase being developed will only be recovered if and when subsequent development is completed. Moreover, because such expenditures increase holding costs, any delay in completing subsequent phases of the project will serve to increase their costs as well. In marginal ventures such cost increases can result in project failure.

Capital

The role of capital as a primary agent of production was first recognized by Adam Smith, who suggested that capital, in combination with land and labor, was a necessary ingredient of a productive good or service. Capital is an important agent of production because it serves as a bridge between expenditures for land and labor and the subsequent receipt of income once a product is sold. Theoretically, if capital were not necessary to pay for the other factors of production, it would be unnecessary to the production process.

In most subdivision developments, capital is derived from two sources: borrowed capital and equity capital. Borrowed capital is supplied for a specific period of time at a specific cost (the interest rate). Equity capital is normally supplied until a development is completed or until it is repaid. The cost of equity capital (the equity yield) may be explicit, but more often it is implicit because the developer and equity investor may be the same individual.

As mentioned earlier, the availability of capital is important because it serves as the financial bridge between cash expenditures and cash receipts. If capital is not available to bridge the time gap between expenditures and receipts, the project will not be undertaken.

Adequate capital is needed to provide a reserve fund to absorb cost overruns, changes in the timing of expenditures, and delays in the receipt of revenues. The adequacy of equity capital is particularly important because it is normally counted on to cover unexpected costs. The stability of capital is crucial because sudden repayment could drain a venture of cash and result in immediate project failure. A primary role of equity capital is to provide financial stability to a venture by serving as a source of additional capital. The cost of both debt and equity capital is significant to a subdivision development because capital costs are directly related to the time period between capital expenditures and the receipt of income.

Frequently subdivision development analysis is undertaken without adequate consideration of financing. In doing so the appraiser assumes that the project is financed entirely with equity capital. With or without special consideration of financing, the value estimate should be the same. Typical financing should be assumed when leveraged analysis is applied. The rate of return, or cost, anticipated for equity capital would generally be higher in a leveraged analysis.

Entrepreneurial Reward

"Without entrepreneurial initiative there can be no real estate or economic activity within the capitalist system."[1] While few would argue that it is the expectation of profit that motivates an entrepreneur to undertake a venture, profit is often the subject of misunderstanding and debate when it is analyzed in the context of a real estate appraisal. Questions relating to real estate profit include:

- Should entrepreneurial profit be added to the value estimate derived in the cost approach?
- Should profit be deducted in a discounted cash flow analysis?
- How should profit be measured?
- When is profit earned?
- Does entrepreneurial profit apply only to the improvements or to the land and improvements?
- Is entrepreneurial profit applicable to all projects or just large projects?[2]

Profit is the reward received for the *successful* completion of a venture: "As used in theoretical economics, the residual share of the product of enterprise accruing to the entrepreneur after all payments for capital (interest), for land (rent), and for labor including management (wages)."[3] Profit is therefore the earnings that an entrepreneur receives after all other agents of production have been paid.

Although profit is considered a residual, it can arise from a number of sources. Equally important, the activities of an entrepreneur may result in profits that are realized in varying amounts at different points in the production process of a good or service. Therefore, several tiers of profit may exist depending on the roles of the entrepreneur.

---

1. Sanders A. Kahn, "The Entrepreneur—The Missing Factor" in *Down To Earth* (Chicago: Society of Real Estate Appraisers, 1985). This article was originally published in the October 1963 issue of *The Appraisal Journal.*

2. Valuation and Evaluation of Proposed Projects, an educational seminar prepared by William L. Pittenger and formerly offered by the Society of Real Estate Appraisers.

3. Society of Real Estate Appraisers, *Real Estate Appraisal Terminology,* Byrl N. Boyce, ed. (Cambridge, Mass.: Ballinger Publishing Company, 1984).

▼▼▼

To measure profit accurately the analyst must recognize that each source of profit in a real estate investment is directly linked to the successful completion of a specific activity, rather than to other profit sources. In a subdivision development an entrepreneur may earn a profit on the equity capital invested, a profit for serving as a general contractor, a profit for real estate brokerage activities, and a profit for coordinating the project.

First, a profit may be earned as a return on invested capital. Capital is a scarce resource that is only supplied if an investor receives compensation for factors such as the risk of loss and a lack of liquidity. A supplier of capital does not need to assume the role of an entrepreneur to receive a return on invested capital; there are usually a large number of competing opportunities available for the investment of capital. Thus, a capital supplier can receive a competitive return on invested capital regardless of the use to which the capital may be put. The return on capital in a subdivision analysis is generally reflected in the interest on debt and the equity yield rate on the equity investment.

Second, a profit may be earned on the construction of site improvements. A general contractor who handles all of the construction work involved with a real estate project normally expects to receive a profit on the work performed. A contractor's profit is expected as a reward for the contractor's efforts whether or not this individual is involved in other aspects of the development. Thus even if the general contractor for the subdivision development is the owner of the project, he will normally expect to receive a profit for this work at least equal to the amount that an unrelated third party would have been paid for the same work. In a subdivision analysis, contractor profit is typically included in the construction costs of the site improvements.

Third, a profit may be earned on the sales effort required to transfer ownership of a development to its ultimate end users or owners. Individuals who engage in real estate brokerage expect to be rewarded for their services. The profit generated from a brokerage operation is separate from the role of the entrepreneur. In a subdivision analysis, a broker's profit is typically incorporated into the sales costs deducted in the cash flow analysis.

Fourth, a profit may be earned for the effort expended to locate a subdivision site, plan the project, secure government approvals, coordinate the construction work and sales effort, and handle other administrative details. Entrepreneurial profit is the compensation a developer receives for these activities. Because these entrepreneurial efforts are independent of any other roles the entrepreneur may assume, entrepreneurial profit is distinct from other types of profit. Entrepreneurial profit should not be viewed as compensation for activities associated with a general contractor, capital supplier, or real estate broker. In subdivision analysis, entrepreneurial profit is typically incorporated into the discount rate or deducted as a line item of expense in the cash flow analysis.

Each of the four types of profit described involve different activities completed at different times. For example, profit on the construction phase of a development may be considered to be earned when all construction work is completed; profit on the brokerage activity may not be earned until the development is completely sold out. The time period when the profit is earned depends on when the particular activity is completed.

To estimate the entrepreneurial reward component of a subdivision development, the analyst should identify each source of profit and account for each consistently. The analysis should reflect the timing of each type of profit in relation to the associated activity. The profit levels considered in the analysis should be consistent with the activities undertaken and the risks involved at various stages of development and sellout.

THE DEVELOPMENT PLAN

Once the appraisal problem has been identified and the analytical process has been outlined, the appraiser should focus on the development plan. The development plan is especially critical when the appraisal involves estimating the value of a development that is not physically complete on the date of valuation.

The importance of determining the precise nature of the development cannot be overstated. Knowledge of the development plan is crucial because the plan will dictate the direction of the analysis. Without a complete plan the appraiser will not be able to determine what information needs to be evaluated or even what property is to be appraised.

Because the development plan will govern the scope of the work to be performed in completing the project, it must include sufficient detail so that all relevant costs can be accurately estimated. Conceptualized plans or artist renderings are rarely adequate.

Most development plans are prepared by professional architects or engineers. The development plan should specify the number of lots, their sizes, and the location of all roads, utility lines, and easements. The plan should also include a full listing of the project's specifications. Amenities such as buffer zones, pools, playgrounds, and other recreational facilities should be clearly identified on the development plans. Detailed plans and specifications should be available for all planned improvements.

SITE PLAN REVIEW AND ANALYSIS

Before a meaningful site plan review and analysis can be undertaken, the appraiser must have access to detailed plans and specifications for the development. In addition, the appraiser must obtain specific information on anticipated costs, project timing, and completion dates. All of this information is needed to form a proper understanding of the plan of development.

Efficient project design maximizes the utility of the site.

Physical Layout

To evaluate the physical layout of a development, the appraiser should note the usable land area and any layout problems that might be evident. An efficiently designed project will maximize the utility of the site by minimizing the negative features of the property.

▼▼▼

This phase of the analysis should focus on

- Lot size and density
- Topographic features of the site and lots
- The existence and location of utilities
- Street size, placement, and profile
- Setbacks and buffer zones
- Water runoff and erosion control
- The location, type, and size of public facilities
- Geologic and soil conditions
- Legal and governmental restrictions on use
- Receipt of all necessary governmental approvals

The boundaries, dimensions, and area of all lots should be clearly identified on the development plan. The plan should also identify the location of all easements. Sufficient detail should be supplied to allow the analyst to determine the impact of easements and lot dimensions on the effective usable area of the site and access to each lot.

The layout of the project's road system should be carefully examined. The interior and access road system provided must be adequate to accommodate the expected traffic within the development and to ensure the safety of its residents. Inefficient road systems can create excess traffic, noise, and pollution, which may be detrimental to the project's success. One excellent method for determining the efficiency of a road layout is to calculate the ratio of linear street footage per lot and compare the figure to the street/lot ratios of competing projects.

The project's road system should be engineered to provide for safe traffic flow and surface water runoff. The project plan should describe in detail the proposed installation of curbs, gutters, and sidewalks and the treatment of storm water runoff. The overall plan of the road network should be accompanied by detailed cross-section and profile maps identifying changes in elevation along roads and the type of construction materials to be used.

The site improvement plans should clearly identify how sewage generated by the project will be handled. If the installation of a public sewer system is planned, a complete outline of the collection and transmission system should be provided. If the plan calls for onsite sewage treatment, it should be accompanied by an engineering report describing the soil's ability to handle the volume of water generated by the project. The project plans should describe the details of the onsite treatment facility and state whether all environmental approvals to operate it have been obtained.

The method employed to supply water to the developed lots should be fully identified, including the source of the water, transmission pipeline specifications, and the location of fire protection lines. The capacity of municipal utilities and the cost of obtaining service should be carefully researched to determine how these factors impact the utility of the site. If the development will rely on private wells, the development plan should be accompanied by an engineering report that examines the availability and suitability of ground water.

In summary, the location and type of all utilities to be supplied to the project should be fully identified on the project plans. The method of solid waste disposal should also be identified in the project's specifications.

Because the topography of the site can have a strong impact on the cost of development, particular care should be devoted to evaluating the topographic conditions present. In describing site conditions, general terms such as *level, rolling* and *hilly* should be avoided.

Elevation changes can be expressed either as changes in the vertical distance between two points located 100 feet apart horizontally or as a ratio of vertical change between two points located 100 feet apart horizontally. For example, the following classification system might be used to describe the topography of a site:

- 0%-2%: nearly level or gently undulating
- 3%-8%: gently sloping or undulating
- 9%-15%: moderately sloping or rolling
- 16%-30%: strongly sloping or hilly
- 31%-40%: steep
- Over 40%: very steep

Project Amenities

Project amenities have become crucial valuation factors in subdivision property. Because amenities can assume many forms, each project must be carefully studied to identify positive and negative design features that could affect the marketability of the subdivision lots. For example, buffer zones to control noise and create an atmosphere of privacy may be established using natural changes in elevation. Certain amenities are not always seen as positive features in the marketplace. For example, public parks and playgrounds may be considered positive features only by the residents who are not located adjacent to them. Adjoining property owners may consider them a nuisance.

The capacity of the amenities to fulfill their intended purpose is an important consideration. Recreational facilities such as public pools and tennis courts should be designed to accommodate the expected usage demands of residents. Inadequate facilities may be viewed by the market as negative factors, while excessive facilities may be expensive to install, operate, and maintain.

Comparison with the Competition

In the site plan review and analysis process, the appraiser compares the planned development to its competition. Each real estate project must compete for buyers with other projects. A typical purchaser normally has a wide array of investment alternatives, so the success of a development will depend largely on its ability to compete successfully for purchasers. Therefore, the ultimate focus of the valuation process must be the competitive position of the property in the marketplace.

Site Improvements

The analyst studies the site improvements to be installed and determines how they will enhance the utility of the site. This phase of the analysis should identify

- The expected cost of the site improvements
- The location and capacity of public utilities
- The location, type, and size of public facilities

- Facilities to handle water runoff and erosion control
- The road network and its ability to accommodate traffic flow efficiently
- Security

Government Restrictions

The last major topic to be addressed in the analysis of a subdivision is the presence and impact of government restrictions on the project. The development plan should clearly indicate whether the project complies with all existing land use regulations pertaining to the improvement type, density, required setbacks, building height restrictions, and parking requirements. If the development plan has not received specific government approval, the appraiser should exercise caution in expressing any opinion as to whether the plan complies with government regulations, unless he or she possesses special expertise in such matters.

In many areas, government regulations require an environmental impact study to address such factors as

- Traffic volume and control
- The capacity of utilities to serve project needs
- Water erosion and runoff control
- The presence of environmental hazards or endangered wildlife
- Significant archaeological sites

Without an acceptable environmental impact study, official approval of the project may be delayed indefinitely. The project may need to be redesigned to satisfy objections raised by private citizens or governmental representatives.

3

HIGHEST AND BEST USE

INTRODUCTION

Highest and best use is fundamentally a simple concept based on the idea
that the worth of an asset is related to its utility. The better, or more useful, the purpose to which an asset can be put, the greater its value. In real
estate appraising this concept has evolved into the practice of appraising a
property based on its highest and best use because this use will result in the
highest present value of the property.

▼▼▼

FOUR TESTS

To better understand how the principle of highest and best use is applied, it is important to recognize that the determination of highest and best use is an analytical procedure. The appraiser subjects the property to four tests to find the use that is legally permissible, physically possible, financially feasible, and results in maximum value for the property.

Legality of Use

Legality is often the first factor considered in a highest and best use analysis. It is a useful starting point because the uses that are legally permissible and those that are not can often be easily distinguished. This criterion may eliminate a wide array of possible uses.

In determining which uses are legally permissible, the analyst does not consider only the limitations placed on the property by zoning codes; environmental regulations, building codes, fire regulations, and title restrictions may be equally important.

In considering the question of legal usage, a troublesome situation arises when a proposed use is not legally permissible on the date of valuation. In deciding whether to consider a change in legal use, two factors should be considered. First, the analyst considers the probability that a change in the legal use can be obtained. A change in use should be reasonably probable if it is to be considered in the analysis. To be reasonably probable there must be evidence to support the assumption that the change will be granted. Typical evidence might be a history of similar changes being granted, a lack of opposition to the change by other parties, or information that the proposed change conforms with, and is a part of, the overall master plan for the community.

Second, the analyst considers whether typical purchasers would base their decision to acquire the property on a change in the legal use. If purchasers would not acquire a property with the expectation that its legal usage could be changed, the change should not be considered in the analysis.

▼▼▼

Physical Adaptability of Use

The physical adaptability of the property for a particular use is often the second factor considered in highest and best use analysis. Physical adaptability is considered after legality of use because once the number of legally permissible uses is established, it is relatively easy to identify those that are physically possible.

The second test of highest and best use, physical adaptability, requires the consideration of site size, shape, topography, access, and view.

In considering the physical adaptability of a site as though it were vacant, the analyst focuses on factors such as size, shape, topography, access, and view. Each of these factors may limit a property's capacity to be put to all the legally permissible uses. The list of possible uses may be restricted by the physical adaptability of the property.

The physical adaptability of a property that is currently improved must also be considered in highest and best use analysis. This phase of the analysis focuses on how the existing improvements will restrict the use of the property. For example, if all the subdivision improvements have been built, it may not be physically practical to change the development plan. Therefore, even if the development plan contains serious design flaws that will affect its marketability, it may not be possible or practical to redesign the development.

Financial Feasibility

The next step in highest and best use analysis is critical: determining which legally permissible and physically possible uses are also financially feasible. In assessing financial feasibility, the following factors should be considered:

- Who will the likely purchasers be?

▼▼▼

- When, or over what time frame, is the property expected to be sold?
- How much is a typical market buyer likely to pay for the property?

A market analysis must be performed to answer these questions properly. Many of the issues addressed in financial feasibility analysis are identical to those studied in market analysis and very similar to those considered in evaluating the economic feasibility and profitability of a project.

Proposed Use vs. Highest and Best Use

In forming a highest and best use conclusion, the analyst should not lose sight of the purpose of the appraisal assignment. If the assignment calls for valuation of a proposed project, then the appraiser's conclusion should reflect the value of the proposed project regardless of whether or not the proposed use is the highest and best use of the property.

One way to ascertain whether a proposed use is the highest and best use of a property is to evaluate the financial feasibility of the use. By definition, the use that is maximally productive is the highest and best use of the property. In establishing whether a particular use is financially feasible, it is important to recognize that the highest and best use is directly related to the purpose of the appraisal. If the purpose of the appraisal is to estimate market value, the highest and best use conclusion will reflect the highest and best marketable use. Alternatively, if the purpose of the appraisal is to estimate value in use, the highest and best use analysis will focus on how well a particular use satisfies the objectives of a specific user or owner.

Establishing the financial feasibility and profitability of a use generally requires that an estimate of value be produced; therefore, this task cannot be undertaken until the appraisal is nearly completed. If it turns out that the proposed use is not financially feasible, the analyst may need to consider other uses for the property to establish the value of the undeveloped site as well as the contributory value of any proposed improvements.

Highest and Best Use Selection Criteria

Although highest and best use is not considered a fact to be found, the highest and best use conclusion can be supported. A properly developed conclusion should assess an improved property from two different perspectives. First, it should consider the property as though it were vacant and available for its highest and best use. In this scenario, it is presumed that the improvements do not exist. Second, the analyst considers the property as it is currently improved. In assignments involving a proposed improvement or use, the "as improved" scenario focuses on the intended use to determine whether it constitutes the highest and best use of the property.

Differences between the "as though vacant" scenario and the "property as improved or proposed" scenario indicate that the improved use is not the optimal use of the property. Such differences should be noted because they may indicate that the data used in the sales comparison and income approaches need to be adjusted for functional and external (economic) obsolescence and that depreciation deductions are needed in the cost approach. (The depreciation deduction would be estimated based on the difference in value between an existing improvement with evidence of accrued depreciation and a proposed improvement without any depreciation.) Differences in use scenarios may suggest that alternative use possibilities should be explored to estimate the value of the raw land.

Another subtlety to be considered in assessing differences between a site as though vacant and available for development and as presently improved is that the former scenario presumes any improvement to the land will be new. This point is significant because some analysts incorrectly assume that if the existing improved use is identical to the highest and best use of the site as though vacant, there is no difference between the two use conclusions. This assumption may be incorrect because if the existing improvement is not new there is a difference, which is directly attributed to the existence of physical deterioration in the existing improvement.

The highest and best use conclusion should be reasonably specific because it will serve as a key criterion in data selection. General use conclusions are not appropriate because they do not facilitate identification of the competitive market. The highest and best use conclusion should be specific enough to assist the appraiser in identifying properties that would be considered competitive with the subject property.

Although it is often assumed that there is only one highest and best use for a property, this is rarely the case. Often a property could be developed in a variety of ways which would result in a maximization of both value and investment returns. Thus it is usually not appropriate to conclude that only one development scheme represents the highest and best use of a property. Rather, highest and best use analysis should focus on whether a given property use reflects an optimal combination of legally permissible, physically possible, financially feasible, and maximally productive attributes.

The highest and best use selected for a property should reflect this optimal combination. If the use conclusion pertains to a vacant site or a site considered as though vacant and available, then the conclusion should reflect a use that is legally permissible, physically possible, financially feasible, and maximally productive. If the use conclusion relates to an existing or proposed use, then it should reflect the highest and best use of the property as it currently exists or in its proposed use.

A highest and best use analysis is a critical part of every appraisal assignment because it sets the stage for the entire valuation process. Once the highest and best use conclusion has been reached, it will govern the type of market data to be selected and the valuation techniques applied to process that data.

4

ANALYSIS OF PROJECT MARKETABILITY

MARKET ANALYSIS

Purpose

The basic purpose of market analysis is to estimate the expected revenues to be derived from ownership of the real estate. The analyst examines both supply and demand factors in the market to estimate the dollar amount of expected revenue flows and their timing.

▼▼▼

Primary and Secondary Data Sources

To assess the marketability of a property, the appraiser gathers data from both primary and secondary sources. The primary data collected by the appraiser relate to the specific market in which the subject property is located. Primary data may include

- Specific property sales information
- Buyer preference surveys
- Project absorption statistics
- Competitive inventory surveys

Secondary data are gathered by others and may include

- Census data
- Information from the Survey of Buying Power
- Building permit information
- Housing and vacancy rates from the Department of Housing and Urban Development (HUD) and postal department surveys
- Surveys and forecasts performed by local planning boards, economic development commissions, and universities
- Multiple listing information
- Surveys by private companies

Identification of the Competitive Market

The first step in market analysis is to identify the market segment in which the subject property is expected to compete. Market segments are typically delineated by geography, product type, and price.

Geographic considerations   Real estate markets are heavily influenced by geographic considerations. One important delineating factor is distance, which can be measured in a variety of ways. Distance is commonly measured in absolute terms—i.e., in miles from one point to another. Nevertheless, absolute distance is often less relevant than travel time by highway or public transportation. In other words, the time needed to travel a given distance may be more important than the actual distance between two points.

▾▾▾

31

Other geographic considerations affecting the delineation of a competitive market include natural amenities such as lakes, rivers, and mountains and man-made features such as railroads and highways. These features may not only limit the size of the competitive market but may also serve as boundaries between market areas.

Other significant locational features such as proximity to shopping, employment, and recreational facilities help further define the competitive area and therefore the market segment of the subject property.

Product type considerations   Because buyers generally have a wide array of housing alternatives, they discriminate by product type. For example, condominium units are not in direct competition with single-family detached residences even if their locations and prices are similar.

Numerous product types are developed in the market because different buyers have different needs and desires. Examples of market segments include young singles, young marrieds, compact families, established families, luxury seekers, empty nesters, active retirees, and retirees interested in retirement or congregate care facilities.

Developers strive for product differentiation by offering slightly different features or amenities than their competitors. Product differentiation may be achieved in a variety of ways; some common strategies involve

- Different lot sizes
- Different view amenities
- Access to community facilities such as churches, schools, public parks, and recreation facilities
- Use of buffer zones to shield properties from adverse influences
- Use of artificial barriers such as golf courses and lakes to create privacy

To assess the competitive position of a residential development, the analyst must understand the variety of product types available and how the subject property compares with its competitors.

Price considerations   Purchasers of residential properties tend to be highly sensitive to price. Houses that sell for prices in the $1 million range are not directly competitive with properties expected to sell for $100,000. To evaluate the impact of price, it is important to recognize that price differences alone do not create a submarket for a development. Market participants must believe that the project offers features and amenities commensurate with the offering prices of the individual homes.

Buyers of expensive homes focus on amenities.

The analyst must understand the motivations of market participants at various price levels. For example, purchasers of lower-priced homes may focus on basic shelter and functional utility, while buyers of more expensive homes have presumably satisfied their basic needs and tend to focus more on amenities.

Supply and Demand Forecasting

Once the subject's competitive market segment has been identified, the analyst considers the expected supply and demand relationship within the market segment.

Market forces Ideally an appraisal should only contain information that relates to the solution of the appraisal problem, and all specific conclusions should be derived directly from the data. Irrelevant information and conclusions that are inconsistent with the data should not be presented in supply and demand analysis or in the final report.

One of the best ways to approach supply and demand analysis is to focus on the market forces that drive supply and demand. Once the underlying forces have been identified, the forecasting process can be divided into two parts: identification and quantification of all known information (existing supply) and identification and quantification of all knowable information

eaking the forecasting process down in this fashion,
e manageable and easier to execute and explain.

The analyst studies both existing supply and sources
of future supply. To estimate existing supply in a market segment, the analyst identifies all properties that compete with the subject property, not just
a sample. Common sources of information about existing property inventory include

- Personal observation and primary research by the appraiser
- Census data
- Building permits
- Local government estimates
- HUD housing studies
- Multiple listing information

In addition to assessing the amount of existing supply in a competitive
market segment, the analyst must determine how long the inventory has
been in existence and how long it has remained unsold.

The second step in forecasting supply is study of the source, amount,
and timing of prospective supply. This analysis should proceed from knowable information. The term *knowable information* is used here because it
helps describe how the forecast will be created.

Much confusion has been associated with forecasting future supply
because the analytic process is often perceived as "crystal ball gazing," or an
attempt to somehow know the unknowable. This perception is inaccurate.
Forecasting is a process in which knowable information is used to arrive at a
logical view of what is likely to happen, but not necessarily guaranteed to
happen, in the future. A forecast links known information to events which
are expected to occur.

A forecast is not a prediction. Predictions require a leap in logic and are
not necessarily based on known or knowable, current information. A prediction does not attempt to show how the future relates to the present. For
example, a clairvoyant does not attempt to link a prediction of future events
to current events. Such a prediction is stated as a fact, independent of and

unrelated to what currently exists. A forecast, on the other hand, links current information in a logical fashion with events that are expected to occur. In a forecast the future is not unrelated to the world as it currently exists or will exist; rather, current and future events are viewed as being inexorably linked in some logical fashion.

Sources of potential new supply information include

- Projects under construction in the competitive market area
- Projects that are planned and have government or municipal approval to begin development
- Projects that are planned or being planned but have not yet been granted government or municipal approval
- Vacant land zoned or included in a master plan for a use that would be competitive with the subject

Each of these information sources involves knowable information, but it is apparent that the reliability of the data declines as the underlying events become less certain. The most reliable indicators of future supply would be projects under construction because it is reasonably certain that these projects will be completed and will compete with the subject. The least reliable information would be obtained from land that is merely zoned or included in a master plan because no one can be certain if or when the land will be developed and become competitive with the subject.

The supply forecast must include consideration of other known or knowable factors that might affect future supply or the timing of its entry into the marketplace. Expected changes in economic conditions can either promote or deter development activity. For example, planned expansion of a local manufacturing plant might increase the future supply and cause it to be developed more quickly than past experience would suggest. Conversely, a pending plant closing might decrease expected supply or delay its entry into the market. Government constraints can also affect development activity.

Once each component of supply has been analyzed, the information gathered can be combined to create a detailed forecast of total competitive supply as well as a detailed forecast of when the anticipated supply will enter the market.

Identifying sources of demand   The process of forecasting demand is similar to supply forecasting. The forces that drive demand must be identified and information must be characterized as known or knowable.

By definition, effective demand is desire backed by purchasing power. That is, individuals can desire things but if they do not have the financial resources to purchase them, there is no demand. This definition implies that demand has two fundamental components: people and income. Demand analysis for a subdivision is undertaken to determine if there are sufficient numbers of people to purchase lots and whether they have sufficient income to do so.

There are five primary sources of demand for housing: growth in the number of households, shift in tenure, replacement of substandard units, overburden of existing households, and pent-up demand.

An increase in the number of households in the market is an obvious source of potential home buyers. Demand due to a shift in tenure arises from households moving from multifamily to single-family homes. Such a shift in demand is typically slow to materialize, so a shift in tenure usually represents only a small portion of the demand for new units. The replacement demand generated by households seeking to move from substandard to standard housing units is also small. Overburdened households that currently occupy units that are too small typically create only minimal demand for single-family homes. The last source of demand, pent-up demand, exists in markets where the housing vacancy rate is below normal.

The stabilized occupancy level selected for use in a supply and demand analysis must be supported with strong market evidence. The common denominators for housing are people, represented by the number of households, and income in the form of household income. Households are studied carefully because housing demand can originate not only from an absolute increase in the population, but also from a change in the number or composition of households. For example, if the average household size is decreasing, demand for additional housing may be produced without pop-

▼▼▼

ulation growth. Household income is also important because it is a key factor in determining the affordability of a housing product. Most housing is purchased with mortgage funds and the mortgage amount is generally limited by household income. Therefore, household income levels are a key variable in forecasting the size of a housing market segment. The use of household and income statistics in estimating market demand is demonstrated in the case study that follows Chapter 5.

Changes in population and household size are focal points in demand analysis. Because employment strongly influences where people live and why they move, this factor is also considered in the analytical process.

Employment in basic industries tends to drive overall employment in the local market. For example, if manufacturing is a basic industry in the market, growth in manufacturing will tend to produce growth in retailing, food, medical, and service industries. The overall level of employment in many markets often depends on basic industry employment.

Current and historical statistics on employment growth and population change are readily available from a variety of reliable sources, including local, state, and federal government agencies, universities, and private vendors. Reliable forecasts of expected changes in employment and population are also available.

Although statistical measures of changes in population and employment are important, this information cannot be translated directly into an indication of demand. The analyst also needs to look at the competitive market segment and forecast how much inventory it can effectively absorb. The following questions must be answered

- How many lots are currently being absorbed in the competitive market segment? How fast are they being absorbed and at what prices? What is the capture rate?
- How many lots have been absorbed in the competitive market segment in the past? How fast were they absorbed and at what prices?
- Why has lot absorption followed this pattern? Is absorption linked to employment in some critical local industry?

- If absorption is linked to a single industry, are there reasons to expect any change in the level of employment in the industry?
- Are any current or future events at the local, regional, or national level expected to alter the demand for lots?
- Has past or current absorption been influenced by any type of sale or financing concession?
- Are there competitive projects under construction or planned that could affect the absorption of the subject units?

Once all questions about population, income, employment, and absorption are answered, a supportable, defensible forecast of demand can be developed.

Correlation of supply and demand   Market analysis must study both supply and demand because it is the relationship between these two forces that constitutes the market. Once key supply and demand information has been gathered, the analyst usually forecasts absorption from two different angles by performing both an inferred analysis of historical trends and a fundamental demand forecast. An inferred analysis, which is generally easier to prepare, is a mathematical projection based on current and historical data from the subject's market segment. The results of this analysis can indicate the relative amount and pace of activity in the market segment. A demand forecast should not be based solely on a trend analysis, however, because potential demand could be significantly overstated or understated should construction and purchasing patterns change due to economic conditions, changes in interest rates or financing, the elimination of tax incentives, or the introduction of a new housing alternative.

A fundamental demand forecast is different from an inferred analysis of trends in that the analyst identifies market factors that could create new housing demand such as growth in population, households, employment, and income levels. The analyst then considers trends in these factors in forecasting the number of new households in the market segment being studied. Next, expected household growth is adjusted for expected vacancy to arrive at potential housing unit demand. Finally, housing demand is adjusted to reflect the characteristics of the market segment. A fundamental demand analysis provides a framework within which the analyst considers many dynamic market factors that exist or are expected to exist in the near future. It is not a static, historical projection like trend analysis.

By estimating demand with both inferred trend analysis and a fundamental demand forecast, the margin for error is reduced.

Relationship between historic and projected supply and demand

One of the most common errors made in forecasting with time series data is to assume that the future will be a mirror image of the past. Although history tends to repeat itself, it is extremely rare for events to be repeated in exactly the same manner.

Forecasts that assume the future will mirror the past are prone to error because they do not see the future as linked with causative factors in a logical progression. For example, a forecast that presumes economic conditions at the peak of a market cycle will continue tends to be unreliable because it does not recognize the cyclical nature of the marketplace. Furthermore, such straight-line projections ignore that the duration of a trend is normally limited.

In evaluating historic supply and demand relationships, an analyst should recognize that the future is more than an extension of the past. Historic relationships change over time, and projections that fail to reflect the complexity of the factors that will affect the market in the future tend to be overly simplistic.

Market share considerations

Another source of forecasting error is the failure to recognize that a new development will be able to capture only a share of the market, rather than the entire market. New projects do not necessarily create new demand. Many analysts incorrectly assume that if there is sufficient demand in the competitive market to absorb five lots per month, a new project will automatically capture all this demand. Competitive projects are ignored or treated as if they will be withdrawn from the pool of total supply until the subject property has been absorbed by the market. Sometimes additional demand equal to total current demand is assumed to arise.

Introducing a new good or service into the marketplace rarely results in total displacement of the demand for other, similar goods or services. Usually the introduction of a new product or service only increases total supply and total demand is redistributed among the existing producers. Over time it may be possible for an exceptionally well-designed product to capture a disproportionate share of the market, but this possibility should not be treated as a foregone conclusion.

Similarly, the introduction of a new good or service in the market does not automatically increase demand. While it could be argued that existing supply is not satisfying current demand, this line of reasoning fails to recognize that a basic need like shelter does not simply go unsatisfied. In most cases the demand for a basic need is satisfied in an alternative fashion—e.g., property rental rather than ownership or occupancy of substandard space. Pent-up demand may not automatically be unleashed when a product intended to satisfy the alleged need is introduced.

Practical limits of forecasting   It is mathematically possible to construct a forecast of infinite duration, but such a forecast will not necessarily be reliable; as the length of a forecast increases, its reliability tends to decline dramatically. Although there are a number of mathematical techniques available to compensate for forecasting error, no method is absolutely satisfactory. For example, forecasting error may be minimized in present value calculations by assigning different discount rates to more distant cash flows in the discounting process.

CASH FLOW FORECASTS

Estimating Revenues

The next step in analyzing highest and best use and project feasibility is estimation of the revenues the subject property will produce. The revenue forecast should reflect the expected pattern of lot absorption over the life of the development as well as the prices lots will likely command.

▼▼▼

The absorption pattern should reflect the likely demand for the subject property in the overall market. Since the subject property will be competing with other housing alternatives throughout the life of the project, the level of demand anticipated for the subject should reflect its relative market share over time.

Similarly, price levels should not be viewed as independent of a specific market. Some analysts erroneously assume that price changes will automatically follow increases in the Consumer Price Index (CPI). This assumption is not realistic. The CPI is a poor measure of real estate price levels because it was designed to reflect changes in the price of consumer goods and services, not real estate. The CPI is based on a hypothetical "market basket" of 250 different goods and services arbitrarily selected by the Bureau of Labor Statistics. The items included in this market basket are not intended to represent typical purchaser demands. In fact, basic items such as housing, employer-financed medical care, and income and sales taxes are not included in the index. Price level changes for items such as tomatoes and video recorders have very little to do with changes in real estate prices.

Real estate prices change in response to changes in the supply of and demand for property. To estimate price changes the impact of increases and decreases in supply must be considered as well as changes in demand. If such changes cannot be reliably forecast, it is not appropriate simply to assume that prices will change in a predetermined fashion. Equally important, price level changes should not be forecast beyond the point when they are likely to occur.

Estimating Project Costs

In estimating the cost to develop a project, appraisers must recognize that cost is time dependent. A cost-of-development estimate is not static, nor is it unaffected by other factors. Because costs change over time, the date of the cost estimate must match the date of valuation considered in applying the other approaches. If the valuation dates used in deriving all estimates do not match, the resulting value indications will not be comparable and may be misleading.

▼▼▼

Expenses for clearing and grading land and installing street improvements are included in site development costs.

Another issue of concern in estimating development costs is which costs should be included in the estimate. Although determining the costs to be included may appear simple, the decision may become complicated by the exact status of the property on the date of valuation.

The costs incurred in the development and sellout of a subdivision are generally divided into three categories: site development costs, marketing costs, and overhead expenses.

Site development costs consist of both direct and indirect expenses incurred to improve the land and create marketable lots. These costs include

- Engineering, survey, and architectural fees
- Clearing, grading, and erosion control expenses
- The cost of street improvements including paving, curbs, gutters, and storm drainage
- The cost of utilities such as sewer, water, telephone, electrical, and gas service
- Common area costs including landscaping, signage, lighting, and amenities
- Indirect costs for permits, financing fees, professional fees, etc.

All of these costs are a function of the overall design of the project and the needs and desires of likely buyers of the finished lots. In forecasting site development costs, care should be taken to ensure that the forecast properly reflects not only the total actual expenses, but also the timing of the expenditures. Often an appraiser is supplied with a cost estimate by the developer. This cost estimate should be cross-checked against the actual development costs of similar subdivisions and perhaps against cost service estimates.

Marketing costs are the expenses incurred to advertise and ultimately sell the lots. Typical marketing costs include

- Advertising and promotional fees
- The costs of marketing materials including sales brochures
- Sales commissions
- Lot closing costs

The marketing costs projected in a subdivision development analysis should reflect expenses typical of the market. Even if the developer plans to engage in the brokerage effort and sell the lots directly, typical marketing costs should be deducted as line item expenses in the cash flow forecast.

The third category of expenses consists of overhead and administration fees. These expenses are incurred to operate and maintain the project during the construction and sellout phases. Typically these costs include

- Real estate taxes and insurance
- Office rent and expenses
- Contributions by the developer to the owners association's operating expenses
- Professional fees

Overhead expenses do not include entrepreneurial profit, which will be discussed later in the text. Although several of the overhead expenses listed are generally paid to the developer, it is appropriate to include a reasonable expense allowance for these items in a subdivision analysis.

The key to proper cost estimation is to estimate all costs that will be or are expected to be incurred in the future. The cost of development estimate should not reflect the theoretical cost to complete the project on the date of the appraisal; the hypothetical cost to complete a development at today's prices may have little to do with the actual costs to complete the project in the future. Moreover, the cost of production should not be based on the historical cost to complete a similar project because such an estimate would not necessarily reflect the costs anticipated for the proposed property.

▼▼▼

One of the best ways to estimate the expected cost to complete a development is to use current bids for the subject project or similar projects. Current bids tend to offer the most reliable information because they reflect current market expectations of future costs. Moreover, recent bid prices require the fewest adjustments because a contractor's bid will incorporate anticipated price increases.

An alternative approach is to evaluate historical cost patterns and current price levels along with inflationary trends and expectations to arrive at the estimated cost to complete a project in the future. When this latter technique is employed, the analyst must schedule price adjustments as the expenditures are expected to occur; otherwise the resulting cost estimate may not reflect the full impact of inflation on the total cost of production.

Entrepreneurial Profit

Perhaps the most perplexing issue associated with estimating costs involves the inclusion or exclusion of entrepreneurial profit. Current economic theory recognizes land, labor, capital, and entrepreneurial reward as necessary agents in the production of any good or service. Although it is clear that all four agents must be contributed to complete a venture, it is not always clear when each plays its role.

In reviewing the sequence of events necessary to create a subdivision property, it is obvious that projects are created by combining the various agents of production over time. Land, labor, capital, and entrepreneurial coordination are invested in varying amounts over the life of a project. As each agent is added to the project, its contribution is reflected as its cost on the open market. The cost of entrepreneurial coordination, however, may be difficult to estimate for a number of reasons.

First, the entrepreneur's contribution is not invested as a capital expenditure. Entrepreneurial reward is an expectation that will only be realized when the market is willing to pay more for the project than the cost of land, labor, and capital.

Second, although significant entrepreneurial effort may be expended prior to completion of a development, it is difficult to measure the amount or timing of the effort invested because very few completed projects are sold in bulk.

▼▼▼

When information on bulk sales is available, the analyst should carefully ascertain the level of compensation paid by the purchasers to the entrepreneur.

Third, the complexity of the development process may vary widely from one section of the country to another. In a rural area, for example, there may be an abundance of land available for development and government approval procedures may be relatively simple. On the other hand, this rural market may be small, which would suggest that most of the risk will be encountered after the development is completed; therefore the major portion of the entrepreneurial reward may be realized during the extended sellout phase. In another area, however, land may be scarce, approvals may be difficult to obtain, and construction time may be lengthy. In this market, demand may be so strong that sellout occurs over a short period and it could be argued that most of the entrepreneurial reward is earned during the construction period. In any case it is essential that the analyst understand the market well before assuming that significant entrepreneurial reward will be earned at the completion of construction. The level of profit allocated at the point of project completion must accurately reflect the risk remaining in the project during the sellout period.

Although there is no simple way to determine how much profit, if any, should be included in the cost estimate, the appraiser might find it helpful to consider at what point developers believe they have earned a profit. Along with the developer's viewpoint, the appraiser should consider whether a purchaser would typically pay a premium to the developer over and above the other three costs of production upon completion or over the course of the absorption period. If this analysis does not indicate that the market would recognize a profit to be earned at completion, then this profit should not be included in the cost-to-complete estimate. If the market would recognize a profit, it should be estimated and included.

TESTS OF FEASIBILITY

Cost vs. Value

The final stage of marketability analysis is to determine whether a project is financially feasible. As noted earlier, the financial feasibility of a project is

▼▼▼

determined with a simple comparison of costs and benefits. If the benefits to be derived from a proposed project are equal to or greater than the cost of production, then the project is considered feasible; if the benefits are less than the cost to produce the project, then it is not feasible.

Total cost of production as a point-in-time estimate   When comparing costs and benefits, the analyst must recognize that both are time dependent. The cost to produce a development can be estimated at various points in time, but typically cost is estimated as of completion.

A cost-to-complete estimate should include only those costs necessary to reach the point of completion. Because certain components of a project—e.g., the land—may have already been acquired on the date the cost estimate is prepared, they will not involve future cash expenditures and are included in the cost estimate at their market value as of the date of completion.

Although a cost-to-complete estimate is not necessarily difficult to develop, questions often arise as to how much, if any, entrepreneurial profit should be included. Minor changes in the allocation and timing of entrepreneurial profit can have a significant impact on the feasibility equation.

Value as a point-in-time estimate   The final element in the feasibility equation is the estimate of the value of the project upon completion. Since this estimate is time dependent, it must be calculated at the same point in time as the cost-to-complete estimate.

The value upon completion is one of the most important figures in the feasibility equation. Regardless of how it is developed, the value-upon-completion estimate represents the worth of the development as a whole on the expected date of completion. Therefore, it is the present worth of the future benefits to be derived *after* the expected date of completion.

Once the value-upon-completion estimate has been developed, it is compared to the cost-to-complete estimate. If the value upon completion is equal to or greater than the cost to complete the development, the project is considered financially feasible. Conversely, if the value upon completion is less than the cost to complete, then the project is considered infeasible.

Threshold Rates of Return

Another common method for determining project feasibility is to compare the internal rate of return generated by a development to the rate of return available from comparable investments. If the subdivision development produces a return at least equal to the minimum threshold rate, the project is considered financially feasible.

Although internal rates of return have been used by financial analysts for years, many appraisers do not commonly employ this technique primarily because of a lack of current information on the investment returns available from comparable properties. A second problem arises due to the relative complexity and variability of the cash flows involved in most real estate investments. Until the recent advent of personal computers, the calculation of internal rates of return from complicated real estate investments was very time-consuming and often difficult to justify.

The two tests of financial feasibility—analyzing cost versus value and threshold rates of return—will be demonstrated in the Forest Oaks Case Study, which follows Chapter 5.

SUBDIVISION VALUATION METHODS

FINANCIAL MODELING SELECTION CRITERIA

To calculate the value of the income produced by a property, the appraiser must select a procedure for converting income into value. Selecting an appropriate procedure is important because it will affect not only the final value estimate, but also the kind of information needed to perform the calculations. Therefore, the financial model to be applied should be selected before data collection and analysis.

Selection of a financial model should be based on three criteria: its ability to replicate reality, documentation and support of all data elements, and the reliability of the forecast.

Ability to Replicate Reality

The primary criterion for a financial model is its ability to replicate reality. Models that do not accurately reflect the expected timing and pattern of cash flows will not produce reliable results.

Ideally the financial model selected should be the one employed by typical purchasers. Models that use analytical techniques similar to those used by a typical purchaser to establish an acquisition price for property tend to produce the best results.

When a variety of models is available or market information does not clearly indicate which model would be employed by typical purchasers, the model selected should be the one that most accurately simulates what is expected to occur.

Documentation and Support of All Data Elements

As a second criterion, the analyst should determine whether all the data required to apply the financial model selected can be properly documented and supported. No financial model, however appealing, should be selected unless all of the data needed to use it can be properly documented and supported.

To decide whether a particular model can be properly documented and supported, the analyst must first recognize that all financial models involve a variety of explicit and implicit assumptions. Simple models are often easier to document and support because they incorporate more implicit assumptions; they substitute assumptions for market data. Unfortunately, these implicit assumptions may not accurately reflect the circumstances of the property being appraised and the value indication derived may be unreliable.

Complex models tend to be more difficult to document and support, but they tend to produce better results than simple models because they require the analyst to address all facets of the subject property explicitly. Even when market data are lacking, complex models tend to produce superior results because they allow the analyst to fill in data gaps with reasoned judgment and logic rather than unsupported assumptions.

Reliability of the Forecast

A third criterion in selecting a valuation model is its ability to produce a reliable forecast. A cash flow forecast can be mathematically projected into infinity, but the forecast produced will not necessarily be useful.

The best financial models reflect reality as accurately as possible and are flexible enough to compensate for both known and knowable forecasting error. Models without sufficient flexibility will not produce reliable results. The amount of forecasting flexibility needed to produce reliable results will depend on the character of the property being appraised and the nature of the appraisal problem.

APPLICATION AND RELATIONSHIP OF VALUATION APPROACHES

To understand the relationship between valuation methods, it is important to remember that the subdivision method represents only one approach to value—i. e., the income approach. Subdivision analysis is not the be all and end all of the valuation process. The cost and sales comparison approaches are applicable to subdivision properties and should be applied as they are in other types of valuation assignments.

Cost Approach

The cost approach is particularly valuable in analyzing proposed developments. The total cost of production is an important measure of the financial feasibility and risk associated with a development. The inability to recover the cost to create a proposed development is not only an indication of economic obsolescence, but also a sign that the property may not be competitive in the marketplace.

Even when an existing subdivision is being appraised, the cost approach is a useful value indicator because it provides information about flaws in the development plan of the project and its competitiveness in the market. The cost approach also offers insight into developers' motivation to produce additional market supply. If a well-designed subdivision cannot recover the costs incurred to produce it, current supply may be excessive relative to demand.

Sales Comparison Approach

Often a lack of market data is the reason given for excluding the sales comparison approach in the appraisal of a subdivision property upon completion but prior to sellout. Even in markets where data are available, it is often argued that past sales were transacted under duress and are therefore not comparable. Although such arguments may have validity, their implications are rarely explored.

One primary reason appraisals are needed is because they represent the only practical means of determining the worth of dissimilar assets that are rarely traded and for which accurate pricing information is difficult to obtain. Thus a lack of readily available market information is not unusual, but quite common.

In the case of a completed subdivision to be appraised prior to sellout, the lack of sales may be due to the absence of willing buyers or sellers for properties at this stage of development. This could suggest that a buyer would be unwilling to pay a price above the hard costs of production or that a developer would be unwilling to part with a project without earning a profit. On the other hand, a lack of sales data could also indicate that a typical developer in the market area expects to both construct and sell out the project lots and would not offer the project for sale after completion but prior to sellout. In this case the scarcity of sales data would not indicate a lack of market activity.

When market sales are lacking, the appraiser must determine why. If the lack of data reflects a marketability problem, the appraiser may need to adjust the profits to be earned for possible sales incentives or for the longer

▼▼▼

51

absorption period required in weak markets. The discount rate may also need to be adjusted to offset the increased level of risk associated with the property.

In markets where sales data are available, they should not be ignored simply because the sales were transacted under duress. The presence of distressed properties in a market may indicate that the overall market is experiencing a slump. Distressed properties may also confirm the hypothesis that entrepreneurial reward should not be allocated to the construction phase of a subdivision development. Market indicators such as these have important implications relative to the application of the other approaches to value and may significantly affect the feasibility of the subject development. Such facts cannot be ignored.

LAND VALUATION METHODS

Sales Comparison Analysis

In a typical appraisal assignment, the value of vacant land can be estimated by direct sales comparison. Sales of vacant land similar to the subject parcel are gathered and analyzed. The sale prices of the comparables are adjusted for the differences in market conditions, location, and physical attributes between the subject and the comparable. Also, if any premium was paid for atypical financing, the sale price of the comparable must be adjusted downward. After considering the reliability and applicability of each adjusted sale price, the appraiser selects a final value indication for the subject property.

Development Approach

The first step in estimating land value using the development approach is to prepare a complete cash flow forecast of the income expected to be received and the costs to be paid by the owner of the land during both the construction phase and sellout period of the subdivision.

The income forecast represents the proceeds from the sale of lots over the anticipated sellout period. In some cases, additional income may be generated from recreational facilities (e.g., swimming pools, tennis courts,

The income and expenses associated with recreational facilities such as golf courses must be recognized in the cash flow forecast for the project.

golf courses, structed as p sion or from maintenance charges. When income from sources other than lot sales is included, the appraiser must be sure that all expenses associated with these additional profit centers are properly recognized and deducted in the cash flow forecast. The costs of development include site development costs, selling expenses, and overhead expenses that will be incurred during the sellout period. In the cash flow forecast, the appraiser must properly identify and include each item of income and expense in the appropriate period. The recognition and allocation of entrepreneurial profit may also be considered. There are several ways to handle entrepreneurial profit in a cash flow forecast. The appraiser may

- Deduct entrepreneurial profit as a line item of expense based on a percentage of sales income.
- Increase the discount rate to reflect compensation for the entrepreneur's contribution in addition to project risk.
- Allocate entrepreneurial profit as a line item expense over both the construction period and the sellout period. Entrepreneurial profit is deducted as a percentage of development costs over the construction period and as a percentage of sales income over the sellout period.
- Deduct fixed dollar payments at various points in the construction and sellout periods of the project.

Theoretically, the techniques used to forecast entrepreneurial profit should not impact the ultimate value of the land because entrepreneurial profit is recognized and supported by the market. The appraiser should select the method that best reflects current market conditions and the behavior of developers in the specific market.

The final step in estimating the value of vacant land when the development approach is applied is to discount the net periodic cash flow forecast to a present value with an appropriate discount rate. If entrepreneurial profit has been deducted as a line item of expense in the cash flow forecast, the discount rate should reflect the return needed to compensate the capital investor for project risk. Typically, if the analysis is undertaken on an unleveraged basis (without the consideration of debt financing), the rate of return would be expected to surpass typical mortgage rates in the market.

The amount of difference between the mortgage rate and the property discount rate is a function of the risk perceived in the project. If financing is included in the analysis, the discount rate becomes the equity discount rate. The equity discount rate is usually higher than the property discount rate because the risk to the equity component alone is greater than the risk to the property as a whole. If entrepreneurial profit has not been deducted in the cash flow forecast, the discount rate used must reflect not only the expected return to the capital invested in the project, but also an adequate provision to compensate the developer for the entrepreneurial effort needed to create a successful project.

Once the discount rate and method for dealing with entrepreneurial profit are selected, the appraiser calculates the present value of the cash flows forecast. The present value calculated is the estimated value of the land "as is."

Financing and the development approach Two types of loans are involved in subdivision analysis: land loans and site development loans. When a land loan is considered in the analysis, it is assumed that the land loan is completely funded as of the date of land valuation and periodic payments for interest and principal will be deducted from the cash flow forecast to satisfy the lender and fully amortize the land loan. The net cash flow after interest and principal payments are deducted represents the net cash flow to the equity position; the present value of these cash flows is the present value of the equity. The land value is the sum of the present value of the equity and the beginning land loan balance.

A site development loan is not funded until the project is underway. The beginning balance prior to commencement of construction is zero and the loan is funded periodically during the construction phase of the project. Periodic payments for interest and principal are deducted from future cash flows to amortize the loan completely over the life of the project. If a land loan has not also been considered in the analysis, the net cash flows represent the return to the land and the present value of the cash flows represents the estimated value of the land. If both land and site development loans are included in the analysis, the net cash flows after deducting the interest and principal payments for each loan would reflect the cash flows to the equity investment in the land; land value would equal the present value of the equity plus the beginning balance of the land loan only.

Frequently a lender makes a loan to cover both the purchase of the land and development of the site. Such loans are typically referred to as acquisition and development loans, or A&D loans. When an A&D loan is considered in the analysis, the appraiser must determine which portion of the loan is provided to fund the land purchase to assess the impact of the financing on the project.

PROPOSED PROJECT VALUATION METHODS

Often appraisers are asked to estimate the prospective value of a proposed subdivision, which is the expected value of the project as of the date of completion (after construction of all site improvements) but prior to the sale of any of the lots. All value estimates derived from the valuation approaches applied should reflect prospective values as of this date. For a single-phase project, the analysis is relatively straightforward. For a multi-phase project, however, the prospective value estimate is typically the expected value after completion of the first phase plus any incremental land value and the additional value contribution of common site improvements to the remaining land. In this case, all the value estimates should be prospective, reflecting value as of the expected date of completion of the first phase.

▼▼▼

e by Sales Comparison

subdivisions are usually not bought and sold upon
ption but prior to sellout. There are, however, exceptions in some
areas of the country. If the appraiser is able to find sales data on projects
sold at completion, the sales comparison approach should be used. To
apply this approach the appraiser must collect pertinent data from each sale,
make appropriate adjustments for dissimilarities in property characteristics
(e.g., density, location, lot size, amenities, market conditions, financing),
and ultimately arrive at an estimate of the value of the project upon completion. This value estimate should be prospective and reflect the expected
value on the projected date of completion.

Prospective Value by the Cost Approach

When the cost approach is applied, the prospective value of the subdivision
is estimated as the prospective value of the vacant land plus the value contributed by the proposed improvements. Again, all estimates should be
prospective and reflect expectations as of the projected date of completion.
The appraiser should make sure that the improvements represent the highest and best use of the site. If market conditions indicate that a portion of
the entrepreneurial reward is earned as of the date of completion, an appropriate amount should be added to the value of the land and the direct and
indirect costs of site development.

Prospective Value by the Development Approach

To estimate the prospective value of a completed subdivision using the
development approach, the appraiser prepares a cash flow forecast of all
incomes and expenses expected after the project is completed. In other
words, the cash flow forecast reflects incomes to be realized and expenses
to be incurred during the sellout period. These net cash flows are then discounted with an appropriate rate to arrive at the value of the project upon
completion but prior to sellout. As discussed in the land valuation section,
the development approach can be undertaken either with or without considering financing. If the report is to be used as a guide in obtaining

financing for a project, it is advisable to consider financing in the analysis to give the lender an idea as to how the financing structure will affect project cash flows.

EXISTING PROJECT ANALYSIS

Frequently, appraisers are asked to estimate the value of subdivisions that are partially or totally completed as of the date of inspection. The methods used are the same as those applied to estimate vacant land value, but for an existing project the value contribution of any improvements must also be estimated. The value of the improvements may or may not equal their cost to date depending on whether 1) the improvements represent the highest and best use of the property and 2) the cost expended represents a reasonable cost for the improvements to date. The appraiser must not assume that the improvements automatically contribute value equal to their cost to date. A feasibility analysis must be performed to estimate the contributing value of the improvements.

Analyzing the feasibility of a partially completed development is extremely complicated for two reasons. First, the treatment of sunk costs can be confusing. Second, the appraisal assignment often includes the assumption that a partially completed property will be completed, even though the project is not financially feasible.

The cost of developing a partially completed subdivision may or may not reflect the value of the improvements.

In evaluating the feasibility of a partially completed subdivision, it is important to recognize that the cost of the development may be unrelated to its worth. Equally important, the amount of money spent on development may not reflect the actual amount of work completed.

▼▼▼

Sunk costs (i.e., the money spent on the development to date) should be considered nothing more than an indication of the amount of money expended, which may have no relationship to value. Therefore, sunk costs should not be considered in the feasibility equation. While the level of sunk costs may indicate that a project would not have been feasible as originally conceived, this does not necessarily mean that the partially completed project should not be completed.

In analyzing a partially completed project, the appraiser focuses on two tasks. First, the current value of the property as though vacant and available for development to its highest and best use should be compared to the calculated "as is" value of the partially completed project, assuming it will be completed. If the calculated "as is" value is greater than the "as if vacant" value minus the cost to remove the existing improvements, then completion is financially feasible. Second, the appraiser should determine if all costs incurred to complete the development will be recovered from the project's expected revenues. If the costs to complete the project cannot be fully recovered, the venture is not considered feasible.

Project Value by Sales Comparison

As mentioned earlier, few sales of partially or totally completed projects may be available in the market, which makes application of the sales comparison approach difficult. It is especially difficult to value a partially completed project with sales comparison because the sale of a partially completed project is usually the result of a development problem such as a shortage of funds, cost overruns, or a lack of market support for the project. If sales data are available, however, the appraiser should gather them, make appropriate adjustments, and arrive at a final value estimate.

Project Value by the Cost Approach

To estimate project value by the cost approach, the appraiser estimates the value of the land as though vacant and ready for development and adds the contributing value of the improvements. Again, the improvements may not represent the highest and best use of the property or cost overruns may have resulted in atypical project costs. The amount of entrepreneurial profit earned to date is also of concern. If the project is incomplete due to poor market conditions or poor planning and significant effort would be required to complete it, it is unlikely that any additional compensation should be allocated to the entrepreneurial effort.

Project Value by the Development Approach

When the development approach is applied, the value of a partially completed project is estimated based on a complete schedule of incomes and expenses for the remaining construction and sellout periods. Income would be derived from lot sales and possibly from owners association dues and the operation of recreational facilities. The costs anticipated would include both the hard and soft costs required to complete the project as well as sales and market expenses, overhead, and entrepreneurial profit. If financing is included in the analysis, any loan advances would be considered a source of income and the principal and interest payments would be cash expenditures. The discount rate used should compensate a typical investor for the risk incurred in completing the project and selling the lots. The contributory value of any excess land or improvements is then added to the present value of the cash flows to arrive at a final value estimate for the project "as is."

If, at this point, the value derived by the development approach is lower than the value estimated by the cost approach, the existing improvements probably do not contribute value equal to their cost to date, which may indicate that the intended use of the property is not the highest and best use of the site. Should this occur, the appraiser should reexamine and verify his or her highest and best use conclusion.

DATA INTERPRETATION AND VALUE CONCLUSION

The final steps in the valuation process are interpretation of the data and formulation of a value conclusion.

The appraisal process should flow logically from problem definition to the final value conclusion. The report should present the process in sufficient detail to allow a reader to follow the analysis from start to finish. When correctly applied the valuation process should result in a logical, defensible estimate of value. If it is employed incorrectly, however, the result may not only be illogical, but also misleading.

In arriving at a final estimate of value, the appraiser should use all applicable approaches to value. By employing more than one approach, significant valuation errors can be avoided. Complete reliance on the subdivision method should be avoided. If, for example, comparable sales indicate that the value of raw land is well below the value indicated by the subdivision method, it would usually be inappropriate to conclude that the value produced by the subdivision method represents a logical, defensible estimate of value.

A similar situation might arise in preparing an appraisal for a lending institution that plans to finance the acquisition and development of a subdivision property. In such a case the subject property will be purchased from a current seller and the acquisition price is an important indicator of value. If the appraiser ignores this price and relies solely on the results of the subdivision model, the final value estimate may be unsupportable because the purchase price may be much lower or higher than the value indicated by the subdivision model.

Another potential problem relates to the treatment of infrastructure in multiphase projects. Often the cost of the infrastructure is divided proportionally among the various phases of the project without considering whether or not the overall development is financially feasible. The contributory value of existing or proposed improvements should not be assumed without a thorough analysis of the complete development plan. If a complete plan is not available for analysis, all infrastructure costs may need to be included in the first phase of the project.

Further problems can be avoided by using consistent terminology. If the purpose of an appraisal is to estimate the market value of a property as of a given date, or at a given point of completion, then the final estimate should be identified as *market value*. Frequently the final value estimate is labeled *wholesale value* or *retail value* even though such terminology may be completely inconsistent with the stated purpose

Appraisers should be aware that users of apprais
familiar with the exact definitions of the terms the
discounted value can be very misleading because it
estimate is somehow less than what the property is actually worth.
Discounting is a mathematical process in which forecast incomes are con-
verted into present value estimates. Therefore, discounted value is not a
type of value, but the result of the mathematical process used to arrive at a
value estimate.

A similar term, *wholesale value*, also suggests a value estimate that is less
than the property's actual worth. Such a term may be meaningless or misleading. Again, if the purpose of the assignment is to estimate market
value, then the final estimate should be labeled market value.

Another terminology problem involves use of the terms *retail value* and
gross sellout value. These terms do not identify value estimates; they represent the total gross receipts expected to be produced by the project. Value
is a point-in-time estimate, based in part on the theory that the value of any
good or service is the present value of the future benefits to be derived
from its ownership. Since arriving at a *gross sellout value* does not involve
consideration of the expenses of disposition or holding or the calculation of
present worth, gross sellout value is not a value estimate. Labeling expected gross receipts as any kind of value estimate is highly misleading and
should be avoided.

Value is estimated at a specific point in time, so an appraisal should
clearly identify when the value estimate is effective. Identifying a prospective value estimate as effective on the date the appraisal is prepared is not
only inconsistent, it is misleading. The prospective value of a completed
development is not realized until the development is completed. Thus the
effective date of a prospective estimate should be the date the value is
expected to be realized, i.e., upon completion of the development.

The schedule used in deriving a gross revenue estimate should present
the income flows when they are expected to occur. The timing of the cash
flows should correspond to the construction schedule and the absorption
forecast.

▼▼▼

Because most revenue forecasts show income as being received on specific dates, the length of time between these dates should be carefully considered. To determine the amount of time between anticipated cash receipts, the appraiser should analyze the scale of the project, the number of sales forecast to occur in each period, the starting date of the marketing campaign, and the amount of time needed to generate sales. Moreover, since each lot represents a distinct product, the number of lots scheduled to be sold each period should be a whole number and not imply sales of partial lots—e.g., 2½ lots, 5.3 lots.

There are no absolute rules concerning how to schedule cash flows (e.g., monthly, quarterly, semiannually, annually). The method selected should have no impact on the final value estimate. The discount rate used to calculate present values, however, should reflect the effective rate for the period selected.

In forecasting cash flows for a partially or fully completed project, it is important to recognize the perspective from which the forecast is being made. The actual timing of cash flows and expenditures may be much different from the timing that may have been forecast for the project at its inception. For example, once a project is completed extra time may be needed to generate sales; thus gross revenues may be realized much later than would have been forecast when the project was proposed. This delay can occur because of a sale. A new owner will usually not begin the marketing effort until the property is purchased. In this case, any previous marketing efforts by the developer would be ignored. This shift in perspective could result in a deferral of sales, a difference in the expected selling prices of the lots, and a different rate of absorption for the development.

In the case study that follows this chapter, the appraiser undertakes the analysis prior to the commencement of the development. Because the project is evaluated from this perspective, it is reasonable to assume that the marketing effort will be initiated well before the development is completed. If there is sufficient time to generate presales, one might even anticipate that some sales could be closed on or before the expected date of completion. In the following case study, however, we will assume that there are no presales.

Sometimes including presales in a cash flow schedule is not supportable or reasonable. If, for example, the analysis is undertaken at the point of completion, it is unlikely that a purchaser could acquire the development, market the lots, find buyers, and close sales on the same day. Because changes in perspective can significantly affect the cash flow forecast and the value of a development, the appraiser should be certain that substantial support exists before including presales in a development analysis.

One issue that frequently arises in developing a cash flow estimate is whether to schedule the cash flows at the beginning of the period or at the end of the period. Many analysts prefer to use end-of-period cash flow models simply because this is how they learned to do present value calculations. Although experienced analysts rarely have difficulty performing present value calculations with beginning-of-period cash flows, less experienced analysts may be unfamiliar with such income streams. To avoid confusion, all cash flows in the case study are assumed to be realized at the end of the period.

Some appraisers advocate the use of mid-period discounting. Mid-period discounting can accelerate the collection of income and thus distort the present value estimate. When it is anticipated that significant income will be collected during the year, the appraiser may have to shorten the period of analysis (e.g., change from annual to quarterly periods) to match income and expenses more logically during the construction and sellout phases of the project.

CASE STUDY—
FOREST OAKS
SUBDIVISION

This case study will illustrate the various processes used to estimate the value of a subdivision "as is" (in this case the value of the vacant land) and the prospective value of the project upon completion. The subject property is a single-phase project with a relatively short sellout period.

   The sales comparison and development approaches are used to estimate the value of the vacant land. In the discussion of the development approach, five methods of arriving at a land value conclusion are presented.

1. A solution in which entrepreneurial profit is deducted as a line item based on 10% of site development costs and 8% of gross sales. A property discount rate is used to reflect the return on invested capital.

2. A second solution in which entrepreneurial profit is built into the discount rate.

3. A third solution in which entrepreneurial profit is deducted as a line item based on 10% of site development costs and 8% of gross sales. Fixed financing of the land is assumed and an equity discount rate is used.

4. A fourth solution in which entrepreneurial profit is deducted as a line item based on 10% of site development costs and 8% of gross sales. A land loan is assumed with a beginning balance based on a percentage of the value of the land and an equity discount rate is used. This method requires an algebraic solution.

5. A fifth solution based on the same assumptions as Solution 3, but with a development loan included to fund the site improvement costs.

The cost and development approaches are used to estimate the prospective value of the property upon completion of the site improvements. Four applications of the development approach are presented.

1. A solution in which entrepreneurial profit is deducted as a line item based on 8% of gross sales and a property discount rate is used.

2. A second solution in which an allowance for entrepreneurial profit is built into the discount rate.

3. A third solution in which entrepreneurial profit is deducted as a line item based on 8% of gross sales. Fixed financing of the project upon completion is assumed and an equity discount rate is used.

4. A fourth solution in which entrepreneurial profit is deducted as a line item based on 8% of gross sales. A beginning project loan based on a percentage of project value is assumed and an equity discount rate is used. This method requires an algebraic solution.

In the development approach analysis, cash flows are forecast on a semi-annual basis and assumed to occur at the end of each period. The analysis does not recognize presales, but assumes that the income from lot sales that

▼▼▼

close after construction are received at the end of the following period. A sample market analysis is presented to support the lot absorption and pricing expectations used in the analysis.

Cash flows are scheduled six months apart because this schedule best reflects the amount of time deemed necessary to complete the development. This schedule also matches the forecast pattern of sales after the development is completed. Thus the interval between cash flows used in this analysis is based on the specific characteristics of the Forest Oaks Subdivision. It should not be assumed that a semiannual cash flow schedule would be appropriate in all situations.

SUBJECT PROPERTY DESCRIPTION

The subdivision being appraised is a small, single-phase project with 55 lots. A brief description of the project follows.

The subject site consists of 27.5 acres which have been subdivided into 55 single-family lots. Lot sizes vary, but the plot plan shows cul-de-sac, corner, and interior lots.

The purpose of the appraisal is to estimate both the value of the vacant land as of January 1, 1993, and the prospective value of the property upon completion of the site improvements but prior to the sale of any of the lots. The site characteristics are described below:

Land area	27.5 acres
Number of lots	55 (single phase)
Average lot size:	
Cul-de-sac	22,500 square feet (18 lots)
Corner	20,000 square feet (9 lots)
Interior	17,500 square feet (28 lots)
Land cost	$500,000 (as of 1/1/92)
Development cost	$550,000
Topography	Rolling, partially wooded
Utilities	All public

Zoning	Residential
Density	2 units per acre
Census tract	10.05
Easements	40-ft. sewer easement
Floodplain	100-year floodplain encroaches on nine lots

Site improvement costs are shown in Table 1.

Table 1—Site Improvement Costs

Item	Unit	Quantity	Unit Cost	Total
Lot clearing	Acre	9	$3,000.00	$27,000
Grading	Sq. ft.	131,600	0.17	22,372
4-in. rock	Sq. ft.	131,600	0.55	72,380
4-in. asphalt	Sq. ft.	131,600	0.80	105,280
1-ft. concrete curb	Lin. ft.	10,200	6.75	68,850
8-in. sewer main	Lin. ft.	3,400	15.50	52,700
4-in. sewer laterals	Lin. ft.	780	8.55	6,669
Sewer manholes	Each	10	1,225.00	12,250
Storm drains	Lin. ft.	3,400	20.00	68,000
6-in. water lines	Lin. ft.	3,400	13.75	46,750
1-in. water laterals	Lin. ft.	780	3.65	2,847
Underground street lights	Each	19	1,420.00	26,980
Underground electrical	Lin. ft.	4,160	2.45	10,192
Erosion control	Acre	27	300.00	8,100
Subtotal				$530,370
Contingency (10%)				53,037
Subtotal				$583,407
Cost multiplier				× 1.00
Current multiplier				× 0.86
Adjusted subtotal				$501,730
Total site improvement cost			Rounded	$500,000
Plus engineering fees				25,000
Plus indirect costs				25,000
Total				$550,000

SUPPLY AND DEMAND ANALYSIS

The following supply and demand analysis for the Forest Oaks Subdivision does not contain all of the data that could have been provided. The series of tables presented here show data on the general market area followed by detailed data on projects in the subject's competitive market segment. The subject neighborhood corresponds to census tracts 10.1, 10.2, 10.3, 10.4, and 10.5.

Supply and demand analysis is conducted to forecast expected lot absorption in the subject subdivision after completion of the site improvements. The analysis is presented in three steps:

Step 1. Analyze population, economic conditions, household growth, and housing type in the general market area.

Step 2. Analyze neighborhood information and generate a housing demand forecast.

Step 3. Analyze competing projects and project absorption for the subject property.

Step 1. Market Area Analysis

Population Tables 2 and 3 indicate that the population of the local area has been increasing. Population growth in the MSA has exceeded state population growth. County growth has remained consistent with overall state growth; city population growth has been minimal due to the limited amount of land available for development within the city limits.

Table 2—Population Growth 1980 to 1990

Year	State	MSA*	County	City
1980	5,085,108	601,272	217,416	135,636
1990	5,889,144	829,146	249,252	141,216
% Change	15.8%	37.9%	14.6%	4.1%

*Metropolitan statistical area

Source: U.S. Department of Commerce, Bureau of the Census, Washington, D.C.

Table 3—Annual Population Growth

Year	State	MSA	County
1990	5,936,400	835,200	243,600
1991	6,014,400	849,600	245,400
1992	6,079,200	874,800	247,800
1993	6,127,800	877,800	251,400
1994	6,217,800	898,200	254,400
Annual increase	1.02%	2.3%	0.9%

Source: *Survey of Buying Power,* Sales and Marketing Management, New York.

Employment   Employment in the county grew approximately 9% from 1990 to 1992. County unemployment fell from 7.2% to 5.4% in the same period. Manufacturing and transportation employment continued to decline, but these losses were offset by increases in the retail trade and service sectors of the economy.

▼▼▼

Table 4—Employment by Category

US %		1990	%	1991	%	1992	%
0.6%	Agricultural	381	0.3%	365	0.3%	394	0.3%
1.2%	Mining	0	0.0%	0	0.0%	0	0.0%
5.4%	Contract construction	5,355	4.4%	5,603	4.6%	7,096	5.4%
24.0%	Manufacturing	44,343	36.7%	45,675	37.5%	48,092	36.6%
6.0%	Transportation	10,710	8.9%	8,770	7.2%	8,672	6.6%
7.2%	Wholesale trade	6,885	5.7%	6,577	5.4%	7,096	5.4%
22.0%	Retail trade	18,890	15.7%	20,097	16.5%	22,075	16.8%
7.2%	Financing, insurance and real estate	7,650	6.5%	7,308	6.0%	7,884	6.0%
26.1%	Services	26,158	21.7%	26,674	21.9%	29,565	22.5%
0.3%	Other	128	0.1%	731	0.6%	526	0.4%
100.0%	Total	120,500	100.0%	121,800	100.0%	131,400	100%

Source: *County Business Patterns,* U.S. Department of Commerce, Bureau of the Census, Washington, D.C.

Table 5—Unemployment

	1990	1991	1992
State	7.8%	7.2%	6.6%
County	7.2%	7.8%	5.4%

Income   Household incomes increased substantial from 1980 to 1990 and county incomes continue to surpass state median and average income levels.

Table 6—Average Household Income

Year	State	MSA	County	City
1980	$ 7,740	$ 8,940	$ 9,000	$ 8,400
1990	$16,890	$18,600	$19,890	$18,900
% Change	118.2%	108.1%	121.0%	125.0%

Source: U.S. Department of Commerce, Bureau of the Census, Washington, D.C.

Table 7—Effective Household Income

Year	State Median	State Average	MSA Median	MSA Average	County Median	County Average
1989	$14,760	$17,910	$17,928	$19,800	$18,932	$20,750
1990	$15,719	$18,985	$18,896	$20,869	$20,066	$21,304
1991	$16,741	$20,124	$19,916	$21,996	$21,043	$23,117
1992	$17,829	$21,331	$20,991	$23,184	$22,991	$24,871

Source: *Survey of Current Business*, Sales and Marketing Management, New York.

Household growth The number of households increased steadily, partially fueled by decreasing household size, which may reflect the nationwide increase in the number of single-parent households during the 1980s and 1990s.

Table 8—Household Growth: 1980 to 1990

Year	State	MSA	County	City	Average Household Size in County
1980	1,475,800	175,200	66,000	42,000	3.29
1990	1,917,630	280,320	89,100	50,400	2.79
% Change	29.9%	60%	35%	20%	

Source: U.S. Department of Commerce, Bureau of the Census, Washington, D.C.

▼▼▼

Table 9—Annual Household Growth

Year	State	MSA	County	Average Household Size in County
1990	2,103,000	303,000	91,800	2.65
1991	2,134,500	309,100	93,000	2.63
1992	2,166,500	315,300	95,300	2.62

Source: *Survey of Buying Power*, Sales and Marketing Management, New York.

Housing type

Table 10—Housing Unit Increase in County: 1980 to 1990

Year	Housing Units	Owner Occupied	Rental Units	% Rental Units
1980	69,900	46,833	23,067	33%
1990	94,365	64,169	30,196	32%
% Change	35%	37%	30.9%	

Source: U.S. Department of Commerce, Bureau of the Census, Washington, D.C.

Table 11—Annual Housing Unit Increase in County

Year	Total Units	% Vacancy	Owner Occupied	% Owner Occupied	% Vacancy
1990	81,550	2.0%	59,532	73%	1.40%
1991	82,997	1.6%	61,318	74%	1.30%
1992	86,217	1.8%	62,292	72%	1.40%
1993	88,923	2.1%	63,270	71%	1.30%
1994	91,286	2.2%	65,250	71%	1.60%
Total change	9,736		5,718	58%	

Source: Survey by the Department of Housing and Urban Development based on U.S. Post Office data.

The difference in the 1990 figures shown in Tables 10 and 11 is due to the fact that the post office data do not include residents of college dormitories, nursing homes, and other group living facilities.

Table 12—Annual Building Permits (in Dollars)

Year	Residential	Multifamily	Total
1988	$31,053,150	$10,558,071	$ 41,611,221
1989	$24,751,500	$14,603,385	$ 39,354,885
1990	$29,254,500	$17,260,155	$ 46,514,655
1991	$63,603,960	$24,169,505	$ 87,773,465
1992	$85,239,300	$28,981,362	$114,220,662

Source: Local building inspection department.

Table 13—Annual Building Permits (No. of Units)

Year	Residential	Multifamily	Total
1988	960	650	1,610
1989	750	1,300	2,050
1990	980	1,600	2,580
1991	1,800	1,500	3,300
1992	2,100	1,850	3,950
1988-1992	6,590	6,900	13,490
1988-1991	4,490	5,050	9,450

Source: Local building inspection department.

The number of housing units increased in direct proportion to the number of households. The most notable trend in new housing construction was the marked increase in multifamily units from 1989 to 1991. By 1992, however, more emphasis was being placed on the construction of single-family units.

▼▼▼

▼▼

Conclusion The county can be described as relatively wealthy with a history of slow, steady growth. No negative trends have been observed in the market over the past several years, so the market appears strong. Two potentially adverse factors that bear watching are the possible oversupply of multifamily housing units and the shift from manufacturing employment to retail trade and service sector employment.

Step 2. Neighborhood Analysis and Housing Demand Forecast

Neighborhood Population and Households

Table 14—Neighborhood Population by Census Tract: 1980 to 1990

Census Tract	1980	1990	Percent Change	Annual Change
10.01	2,778	2,695	−3.0%	−0.3%
10.02	3,560	3,133	−12.0%	−1.2%
10.03	2,970	2,756	−7.2%	−0.7%
10.04	3,462	5,331	54.0%	5.4%
10.05	7,270	8,903	42.0%	4.2%
Total	19,040	22,818	19.8%	2.0%

Source: U.S. Department of Commerce, Bureau of the Census, Washington, D.C.

▼▼▼

Table 15—Neighborhood Households by Census Tract: 1980 to 1990

Census Tract	1980	1990	Percent Change	Annual Change
10.01	1,110	1,210	9.0%	0.9%
10.02	1,176	1,211	3.0%	0.3%
10.03	984	1,087	10.5%	1.1%
10.04	1,164	2,677	130.0%	13.0%
10.05	1,818	3,018	66.0%	6.6%
Total	6,252	9,203	47.2%	4.7%

Source: U.S. Department of Commerce, Bureau of the Census, Washington, D.C.

Two of the five census tracts (10.04 and 10.05) showed exceptional growth from 1980 to 1990; tract 10.05 includes the subject property. Census tracts 10.01, 10.02, and 10.03 experienced decreases in population due to the fact that these neighborhoods are fully developed. The number of households grew significantly faster than the population, which indicates that the average household size was decreasing. Housing demand should have been strong from 1980 to 1990.

Table 16—Neighborhood Housing Units by Census Tract: 1980 to 1990

Census Tract	1980	1990	Percent Change	Annual Change
10.01	1,032	1,156	12.0%	1.2%
10.02	1,086	1,200	10.5%	1.1%
10.03	918	1,028	12.0%	1.2%
10.04	1,170	2,469	111.0%	11.1%
10.05	1,830	2,928	60.0%	6.0%
Total	6,036	8,781	45.5%	4.6%

Source: U.S. Department of Commerce, Bureau of the Census, Washington, D.C.

Table 17—Neighborhood Housing by Zip Code Area*

Year	Total Units	Percent Vacant	Single-Family Units	Percent Vacant
1988	8,940	1.6%	5,900	4.20%
1989	9,003	1.3%	6,001	2.40%
1990	9,308	1.3%	6,148	3.20%
1991	9,498	1.2%	6,277	3.30%
1992	9,716	2.0%	6,413	1.80%
Total change	776		513	
% change	8.7%		8.7%	

Source: Survey by the Department of Housing and Urban Development based on U.S. Post Office data

*Note. Zip code areas and census tracts overlap, but do not match each other exactly.

The postal zip code data indicate that new housing units have increased approximately 8.7% since 1988.

Table 18—Neighborhood Housing Prices and Income Levels by Census Tract: 1990

Census Tract	Median House Price	% Owner Occupied	Median Household Income	Mean Household Income
10.01	$88,800	85.5%	$31,350	$42,000
10.02	$78,000	92.0%	$32,500	$45,750
10.03	$72,000	85.5%	$30,500	$38,500
10.04	$42,000	36.0%	$16,000	$18,000
10.05	$79,350	72.0%	$30,228	$36,000

Source: U.S. Department of Commerce, Bureau of the Census, Washington, D.C.

Economic indicators for the neighborhood are strong. Predominate median house prices range from $72,000 to $88,800 and predominate median household incomes range from $30,228 to $32,500.

▼▼▼

The declining population rates in Census Tracts 10.01, 10.02, and 10.03 appear to be the result of grown children leaving the family home. High median incomes and house prices are reflected in these neighborhoods of empty nesters.

Housing Demand Forecast 1. Trend analysis Careful analysis of Tables 11 and 17 indicates that average annual growth rates over the past five years were approximately 3% for the county and 2.1% for the neighborhood. By applying these growth rates to the previous year's housing stock, demand can be estimated for the next three years. (See Table 19.)

Table 19 indicates that the neighborhood demand for single-family homes is estimated to range from 135 to 140 units per year for the next three years, assuming an annual growth rate of 2.1%.

Housing Demand Forecast 2. Household growth analysis According to *Sales and Marketing* magazine, the number of county households increased from 91,800 to 95,300 between 1990 and 1992. This reflects an increase of 3,500 households, or an average growth of 1,750 per year. The projected growth from 1991 to 1992 was 2,300, which is higher than the average. Housing demand is largely a function of household growth and vacancy. Thus, assuming annual household growth of 2,000 and a 5% vacancy rate, the total annual demand for new housing of all types can be calculated.

$$\text{Household growth} \ /(1 - \text{vacancy rate}) = \text{county housing units}$$
$$2{,}000 \ / \ (1 - 0.05) = 2{,}105$$

This level of demand is slightly lower than the demand indicated by the figures shown in Table 11 (9,736/4 = 2,434 per year), but there was significant construction of multifamily units during this period.

The ratio of owner-occupied housing to total housing in the county is approximately 70%, but only about 58% of the new construction from 1988 to 1992 was of single-family units (see Table 11). This trend appears to be changing. Of the 2,363 units built in 1992, 1,980, or 84%, were single-family. For forecasting purposes, a ratio of approximately 70% will be assumed for the next few years.

Table 19—Trend Analysis

Year	From Table 11 County Housing — Total Units	Growth Rate	Owner-Occupied	Growth Rate	From Table 17 Neighborhood Housing — Total Units	Growth Rate	Single-Family	Growth Rate
1988	81,550		59,532		8,940		5,900	
1989	82,997	1.8%	61,318	3.0%	9,003	0.7%	6,001	1.7%
1990	86,217	3.9%	62,292	1.6%	9,308	3.4%	6,148	2.5%
1991	88,923	3.1%	63,270	1.6%	9,498	2.0%	6,277	2.1%
1992	91,286	2.7%	65,250	3.1%	9,716	2.3%	6,413	2.2%
Total change	9,736	2.9%	5,718	2.3%	776	2.1%	513	2.1%
% change		11.9%		9.6%		8.7%		8.7%
1993	94,025	3.0%	67,208	3.0%	9,920	2.1%	6,548	2.1%
1994	96,845	3.0%	69,224	3.0%	10,128	2.1%	6,686	2.1%
1995	99,751	3.0%	71,300	3.0%	10,341	2.1%	6,826	2.1%

Estimated Unit Demand

County

Year	Total — Total	Total — Units/Yr.	Single-Family — Total	Single-Family — Units/Yr.
1993	94,025	2,739	67,208	1,958
1994	96,845	2,820	69,224	2,016
1995	99,751	2,906	71,300	2,076

Neighborhood

Year	Total — Total	Total — Units/Yr.	Single-Family — Total	Single-Family — Units/Yr.
1993	9,920	204	6,548	135
1994	10,128	208	6,686	138
1995	10,341	213	6,826	140

Now the demand for single-family units in the county can be calculated.

Total demand × % single-family = county single-family demand
2,105   ×   0.70   = 1,473

The last element to be considered is the percentage of single-family demand expected in the subject neighborhood. Of the single-family units built from 1988 to 1992, approximately 9% were built in the subject neighborhood. This percentage is calculated using the neighborhood single-family housing figure from Table 17 and the county single-family housing figure from Table 11 (513/5,718 = 0.09). There is no evidence that this trend will change, so this percentage can be used to estimate annual single-family demand in the neighborhood.

County single-   neighborhood   neighborhood single-
family demand ×   percentage   =   family demand
1,473   ×   0.09   =   133 units

Both housing demand forecasts suggest annual neighborhood demand of 130 to 140 units. Often, however, trend analysis and household growth analysis produce different answers. If different absorption rates are indicated, greater emphasis should be placed on the second method of deriving demand.

Step 3. Analysis of Competing Projects and Project Absorption

History of competing subdivisions Table 20 indicates that competing subdivisions in the neighborhood have had absorption rates ranging from 1.67 to 2.5 lots per month, or between 20 and 30 per year. The annual absorption of subdivision lots in the neighborhood is shown in Table 21. Table 22 provides information on specific subdivision lot sales.

Table 20—Historical Data on Neighborhood Subdivisions

Project	No. of Lots	Year of Completion	Lots Sold	Average Price	Absorption Period	Lots Per Month
Subdivision 1	60	1987	60	$30,000	24 months	2.50
Subdivision 2	42	1989	40	$31,000	18 months	2.22
Subdivision 3	54	1990	54	$34,000	31 months	1.75
Subdivision 4	30	1991	30	$40,000	14 months	2.14
Subdivision 5	48	1992	20	$35,000	12 months	1.67
Total	234		204			

Table 21—Annual Lot Absorption

Year	Subdivision 1	Subdivision 2	Subdivision 3	Subdivision 4	Subdivision 5	Totals
1987	28	0	0	0	0	28
1988	29	0	0	0	0	29
1989	3	24	0	0	0	27
1990	0	16	20	2	0	38
1991	0	0	20	20	5	45
1992	0	0	14	8	15	37

Table 22—Competitive Lot Sales

Project	No. of Lots	Price	Date	Size (in Sq. Ft.)	Price/ Sq. Ft.	Type
Subdivision 4	24	$34,500	1991	20,000	$1.73	Wooded/corner
Subdivision 4	12	$36,000	1991	22,500	$1.60	Wooded/cul-de-sac
Subdivision 4	18	$33,500	1991	19,000	$1.76	Wooded/corner
Subdivision 4	6	$31,000	1991	17,000	$1.82	Open/interior
Subdivision 5	30	$33,000	1992	18,000	$1.83	Open/interior
Subdivision 5	42	$38,500	1992	23,000	$1.67	Wooded/cul-de-sac
Subdivision 5	24	$34,000	1992	19,500	$1.74	Wooded/corner
Subdivision 5	36	$38,000	1992	23,000	$1.65	Wooded/cul-de-sac

Table 23—Lot Prices for Subject Property

No. of Lots	Type of Lot	Average Size	Price/ Sq. Ft.	Price	Price (Rounded)	Sellout
18	Cul-de-sac	22,500	$1.67	$37,600	$37,500	$ 675,000
9	Corner	20,000	$1.75	$35,000	$35,000	$ 315,000
28	Interior	17,500	$1.85	$32,400	$32,500	$ 910,000
55	Total/average	19,500	$1.77		$34,500	$1,900,000

The data in Table 22 indicate the following price ranges for lots:

Cul-de-sac lots	$1.60 to $1.67 per square foot
Corner lots	$1.73 to $1.76 per square foot
Interior lots	$1.82 to $1.83 per square foot

Using this information lot prices for the subject subdivision can be estimated. Table 23 indicates that lots in the subject subdivision will be priced from $32,500 to $37,500.

Forecast Absorption Rate Table 24 shows household income in the neighborhood broken down by census tract. The forecast of effective household income presented in Table 7 shows that the average income in the county increased from $21,304 to $24,871 between 1990 and 1992, indicating a total increase of 16.7%, or 8.0% per year compounded. Assuming that incomes in the neighborhood have grown proportionately, Table 24 indicates that about 49% (16.0% + 15.8% + 17.3%) of the households should have incomes above $31,500, which is $25,000 increased by 8.0% per year for three years ($25,000 \times [1.08]^3$).

If home buyers can spend 25% of their gross household income on mortgage payments (principal plus interest), the high-income households in the neighborhood should be able to make mortgage payments of $656 per month. Assuming an 8.5%, 30-year, fixed-rate mortgage with an 80% loan-to-value ratio, buyers who can make these mortgage payments can afford homes selling for more than $106,000.

Houses built on lots costing between $30,000 and $37,500 generally sell for prices in the $100,000–$150,000 price range. This suggests that at least 49% of the households in the neighborhood could afford homes in the subject subdivision's price range. Because households with incomes below $10,000 (13.3% of the neighborhood households) are generally not in the market for owner-occupied housing, approximately 57% (49% / 86.7%) of the people in the market for housing could afford the subject lots. About 17.3% of these households will have incomes of more than $63,000 ($50,000 \times [1.08]^3$) per year, however, and they could purchase houses

Table 24—Household Income in Neighborhood by Census Tract: 1990

Income Ranges	U. S. Census Tracts						Total	% of Total
	10.01	10.02	10.03	10.04	10.05			
Less than $5,000	40	18	35	175	83		351	4.0%
$ 5,000 - $ 7,499	38	45	45	155	75		358	4.1%
$ 7,500 - $ 9,999	52	66	38	215	89		460	5.2%
$10,000 - $14,999	86	80	125	575	295		1,161	13.2%
$15,000 - $19,999	145	115	99	525	315		1,199	13.7%
$20,000 - $24,999	75	104	89	375	300		942	10.7%
$25,000 - $34,999	230	230	152	215	581		1,408	16.0%
$35,000 - $49,999	198	218	240	125	605		1,386	15.8%
$50,000 and above	292	325	205	109	585		1,516	17.3%
Totals	1,156	1,201	1,028	2,469	2,928		8,781	100.0%

Source: U.S. Department of Commerce, Bureau of the Census, Washington, D.C.

▼▼▼

83

priced above $150,000, outside the price range for the subject property. Consequently, the market size for the development is actually (16.0% + 15.8%) / 86.7%, or 37% of 140 units, which equals 52 units per year. Note that this figure is only slightly higher than the average number of lots sold each year in the competitive subdivisions in the market (see Table 21).

The historical data on neighborhood subdivisions shown in Table 20 reveal that the typical new subdivision has 40 to 50 lots. The subject is scheduled to have 55 lots, a good amount given the market data. An absorption rate of 1.75 to 2.5 per month appears to be supportable. This rate indicates that 21 to 30 units will be sold each year and the subject project could capture between 40% and 50% of the market segment. These estimates seem reasonable in light of the market data and the history of the competitive projects.

Given the level of recent sales in the competitive subdivisions and the economic strength of the subject neighborhood, it is reasonable to forecast that the subject will capture 40% to 50% of the demand for new housing in the market segment, or about 20% of the total demand for lots in the neighborhood. This equates to approximately 25 to 30 units per year, 13 to 14 units per semiannual period, or 2.25 units per month.

LAND VALUATION

Sales Comparison Analysis

In most appraisal assignments land value can be estimated by sales comparison. To apply this approach, sales of vacant land considered similar to the subject parcel are gathered and analyzed. Then adjustments are made to the sale price of each comparable based on differences between the market conditions, location, and physical attributes of the subject and the comparable. Any premium paid for atypical financing also requires an adjustment to the sale price of the comparable. After all necessary adjustments are made, the appraiser assesses the reliability and applicability of each value indication reached and derives a final value estimate for the subject property.

Data on three vacant land sales comparable to the subject property are presented in Table 25. These sales are adjusted and indicated prices are shown in Table 26.

▼▼▼

Table 25—Comparable Vacant Land Sales

Project	No. of Acres	Date	Sale Price	Price/Acre	Comments
Subd. 4	14.8	05/15/90	$250,000	$16,892	Private, good topography
Subd. 5	22.6	03/30/92	$370,000	$16,372	All utilities, average topography
Subd. 6	29.47	11/14/92	$530,000	$17,966	All utilities, average topography plus on-site lake

Table 26—Comparison and Adjustment of Land Sales Data

	Subdivision 4	Subdivision 5	Subdivision 6
Price/acre	$16,892	$16,372	$17,966
Adjustments:			
Time (7%) per year	+12%	+ 8%	+ 2%
Adjusted price	$18,919	$17,682	$18,325
Location	0	+ 10%	+ 5%
Size	+ 5%	0	0
Topography	0	+ 5%	+ 5%
Utilities	0	0	0
Net adjustment	+ 5%	+ 15%	+10%
Indicated price/acre	$19,865	$20,334	$20,158

Based on these data, the land value for the subject property can be estimated at $20,000 per acre, or $550,000 for the 27.5-acre site (27.5 × $20,000 = $550,000).

Development Approach

Five applications of the development approach to land valuation are presented:

1. Land value—no financing
2. Land value—no deduction for entrepreneurial profit
3. Land value with a land loan

▼▼▼

4. Land value—variable land loan amount
5. Land value with a land loan and a site improvement loan

Land Value—No Financing   The following land valuation does not include the consideration of financing. To estimate land value with the development approach, the appraiser first prepares a complete cash flow forecast of the income to be received and the expenses to be incurred by the owner of the land during construction and sellout of the subdivision. The following assumptions apply to the subject property and the cash flow forecast.

- All lots will be constructed in the first six months of project development.
- Thereafter, 13 to 15 lots should be absorbed in each semiannual period. (See conclusions presented on page 84.)
- Total sellout should be accomplished in four periods, or two years, after completion of construction.

Data relating to the planned development of the subject subdivision are presented in Tables 27, 28, and 29.

Table 27—Sales and Construction Schedule

Semiannual period beginning	1/93	7/93	1/94	7/94	1/95
Beginning balance	0	55	40	26	13
Construction period					
Cul-de-sac lots	18	0	0	0	0
Corner lots	9	0	0	0	0
Interior lots	28	0	0	0	0
Total construction	55	0	0	0	0
Sales period					
Cul-de-sac lots	0	5	5	4	4
Corner lots	0	3	2	2	2
Interior lots	0	7	7	7	7
Total sales	0	15	14	13	13
Cumulative sales	0	15	29	42	55

▼▼▼

Table 28—Lot Pricing

Period beginning	7/93	7/94
Cul-de-sac lots	$37,500	$38,750
Corner lots	$35,000	$36,000
Interior lots	$32,500	$33,500

Note. Lot prices were increased approximately 3% after the first year.

Table 29—Schedule of Costs

Land cost	$500,000 (appraised value of $550,000 as of 1/93)
Indirect costs	$25,000
Engineering fees	$25,000
Development costs	$500,000 (allocated over 6 months)
Sales commissions	10% of sales
Sales expenses	$350 per lot sold
Marketing expenses	1% of sales
Overhead	$7,500 per quarter
Real estate taxes	$300 per remaining lot
Entrepreneurial profit	8% of sales income; 10% of site development costs
Construction period	6 months

Using the sales and construction, lot pricing, and cost information in these tables, the cash flow forecast shown in Table 30 is developed. Note that in the cash flow tables that follow, the first column, identified as cash flows for the semiannual period beginning 1/1/93, shows cash flows that are assumed to be recognized as of 6/30/93.

Table 30—Net Cash Flows

Semiannual period beginning	1/93	7/93	1/94	7/94	1/95	Totals
Source of cash						
Sales income (lots)						
Cul-de-sac	0	$187,500	$187,500	$155,000	$155,000	$ 685,000
Corner	0	105,000	70,000	72,000	72,000	319,000
Interior	0	227,500	227,500	234,500	234,500	924,000
Total	$ 0	$520,000	$485,000	$461,500	$461,500	$1,928,000
Total cash	$ 0	$520,000	$485,000	$461,500	$461,500	$1,928,000
Use of cash						
Development costs						
Indirect costs	$ 25,000	0	0	0	0	$ 25,000
Engineering fees	25,000	0	0	0	0	25,000
Development costs	500,000	0	0	0	0	500,000
Total	$550,000	$ 0	$ 0	$ 0	$ 0	$ 550,000
Selling costs						
Sales costs	$ 0	$ 52,000	$ 48,500	$ 46,150	$ 46,150	$ 192,800
Sales expenses	0	5,250	4,900	4,550	4,550	19,250
Marketing expenses	0	5,200	4,850	4,615	4,615	19,280
Total	$ 0	$ 62,450	$ 58,250	$ 55,315	$ 55,315	$ 231,330
Admin./overhead						
Overhead	$ 15,000	$ 15,000	$ 15,000	$ 15,000	$ 15,000	$ 75,000
Real estate taxes	500	14,250	9,900	5,850	1,950	32,450
Total	$ 15,500	$ 29,250	$ 24,900	$ 20,850	$ 16,950	$ 107,450
Entrepreneurial profit	$ 55,000	$ 41,600	$ 38,800	$ 36,920	$ 36,920	$ 209,240
Total costs	$620,500	$133,300	$121,950	$113,085	$109,185	$1,098,020
Net cash flow	−$620,500	$386,700	$363,050	$348,415	$352,315	$ 829,980

The next step is to select a discount rate and apply it to the net cash flows to arrive at an estimate of the present value of the land (see Table 31). In this example, a 15% property discount rate was used, which equals 7.5% on a semiannual basis.

Table 31—Discounting Cash Flows to Present Value

Semiannual Period Beginning	Cash Flow		PV Factor @ 7.5%	Present Value
1/93	−$620,500	×	0.93023	−$577,208
7/93	$386,700	×	0.86533	334,623
1/94	$363,050	×	0.80496	292,241
7/94	$348,415	×	0.74880	260,893
1/95	$352,315	×	0.69656	$245,409
Total				$555,958

Summary of Findings

- Assuming a 15% property discount rate, the present value of the land is $555,958.
- The effective date of the appraisal of the vacant land is January 1, 1993, which is immediately prior to the start of the six-month construction period.
- The cash flow forecast covers five semiannual periods.
- Incomes and expenses are included in the forecast when they are expected to occur.
- The effective property discount rate for each six-month period is 7.5% (15% / 2).
- Entrepreneurial profit is estimated at 10% of site development costs and 8% of sales income for each period. These rates reflect current market expectations.

Land Value—No Deduction for Entrepreneurial Profit

Table 32 shows land value estimation using the development approach with no line item deduction for entrepreneurial profit. When the property discount rate is increased to 27% and entrepreneurial profit is eliminated as a line item of expense, the present value of the land is estimated to be $547,918, very close to the $555,958 estimated using the 15% discount rate and the 10% and 8% entrepreneurial profit percentages.

In this case the rate of return, or discount rate, represents a return on the invested capital plus compensation to the entrepreneur for the effort expended to create the project.

Land Value with a Land Loan　Land value can also be estimated assuming typical financing of the land purchase. The loan amount is deducted from the total value of the land to arrive at the value of the equity investment in the land. The interest and principal payments on the loan are deducted from the periodic cash flows. When a loan is included in the analysis, the applicable discount rate is not the property discount rate, but the equity yield rate. Tables 33 and 34 illustrate a typical land loan payment schedule, assuming the following terms:

Loan amount	$400,000
Interest rate	11% (5.5% per semiannual period)
Repayment terms	125% (loan payments as percentage of unit sales)

Note: Interest based on average loan balance

To arrive at a land value estimate similar to the estimate derived when no financing was assumed ($555,958), the discount rate was increased from 15% to 18%: this rate now represents an equity yield rate. If the property discount rate of 15% were used, the value estimate would have been $585,706, about $30,000 higher. Since borrowing money creates additional risk for the landowner, it would be inappropriate not to increase the discount rate when financing is included in the analysis. In this case, increasing the discount rate by 3% produced a virtually identical land value

▼▼▼

Table 32—Net Cash Flows

Semiannual period beginning	1/93	7/93	1/94	7/94	1/95	Totals
Source of cash						
Sales income	$ 0	$520,000	$485,000	$461,500	$461,500	$1,928,000
Total cash	$ 0	$520,000	$485,000	$461,500	$461,500	$1,928,000
Use of cash						
Development costs	$550,000	$ 0	$ 0	$ 0	$ 0	$ 550,000
Selling costs	0	62,450	58,250	55,315	55,315	231,330
Admin./overhead	$ 15,500	$ 29,250	$ 24,900	$ 20,850	$ 16,950	$ 107,450
Total costs	$565,500	$ 91,700	$ 83,150	$ 76,165	$ 72,265	$ 888,780
Net cash flow	–$565,500	$428,300	$401,850	$385,335	$389,235	$1,039,220
PV of cash flow	–$498,238	$332,473	$274,838	$232,196	$206,649	$ 547,918
Value	$547,918					
Annual *IRR*	0.2700					

▼▼▼

91

Table 33—Land Loan Payment Schedule

Period	1	2	3	4	5
Percent of unit sales	0	27.273%	25.455%	23.636%	23.635%
125% of unit sales	0	34.091%	31.818%	29.546%	*4.545%
Beginning loan balance	$400,000	$400,000	$263,636	$136,363	$18,181
Principal payment	0	136,364	127,273	118,182	18,181
Ending loan balance	$400,000	$263,636	$136,363	$ 18,181	$ 0
Average loan balance	$400,000	$331,818	$200,000	$ 77,272	$ 9,090
Interest payment	$ 22,000	$ 18,250	$ 11,000	$ 4,250	$ 500

*Percentage of loan balance outstanding going into the last period

estimate, which suggests that the financing increased the risk to the investor by 3%.

Note that borrowing money at typical loan terms does not create additional value. Thus when the development approach is used, care must be taken to understand how financing affects the yield rates selected by the appraiser. In this analysis, the implied loan-to-value ratio is 71.9% ($400,000 / $556,392).

Entrepreneurial Profit In a subdivision appraisal there are no clear-cut rules concerning entrepreneurial profit. The appraiser may decide to include entrepreneurial profit as a line item expense or to reflect it in the discount rate, or entrepreneurial profit may be excluded from the analysis altogether.

There are two types of profit to be earned from the development and sale of subdivision lots. The first and easiest to understand is the return required to satisfy the passive investor whose only desire is to earn a competitive rate of return on the capital invested. This individual provides the capital, but takes no active part in the management of the enterprise. As in other income-producing property investments, a passive investor may be required to pay operating or management expenses, which would be deducted before any return on the invested capital is received. In a subdivision appraisal, it can also be assumed that a lender will provide part of this investment capital. If so, the interest and principal payments to the lender

Table 34—Net Cash Flows

Semiannual period beginning	1/93	7/93	1/94	7/94	1/95	Totals
Source of cash						
Sales income	$ 0	$520,000	$485,000	$461,500	$461,500	$1,928,000
Total cash	$ 0	$520,000	$485,000	$461,500	$461,500	$1,928,000
Use of cash						
Development costs	$550,000	$ 0	$ 0	$ 0	$ 0	$ 550,000
Selling costs	0	62,450	58,250	55,315	55,315	231,330
Admin./overhead	15,500	29,250	24,900	20,850	16,950	107,450
Entrepreneurial profit	55,000	41,600	38,800	36,920	36,920	209,240
Interest on land loan	22,000	18,250	11,000	4,250	500	56,000
Principal on land loan	0	136,364	127,273	118,182	18,181	400,000
Total costs	$642,500	$287,914	$260,223	$235,517	$127,866	$1,554,020
Net cash flow	–$642,500	$232,086	$224,777	$225,983	$333,634	$ 373,980
PV of cash flow	–$589,450	$195,342	$173,569	$160,092	$216,839	$ 156,392
Value	$556,392					
Annual *IRR*	0.180000					
Equity	$156,392					
Land loan	$400,000					

required to amortize the loan would also be deducted before any return to the passive investor. In this regard appraising a subdivision is similar to appraising an office building using a mortgage-equity analysis. Subdivision analysis is different because 1) the loan, if applicable, may be amortized more quickly over the sellout period; 2) there are generally no proceeds from a forecast reversion; and 3) the required rate of return (or equity yield rate with financing) may be different due to the risk of the project. The profit earned for passive investment is often referred to as the *return on capital.*

The second type of profit is referred to as *developer's profit* or *entrepreneurial profit.* It represents monetary compensation for the time and effort expended to initiate a development and follow through to its successful completion. The developer begins to earn this profit at project inception. The returns grow as the land is bought, plans are drawn up, approvals are received, financing is secured, construction bids are let, construction is begun and ultimately completed, and the lots are sold. It is difficult to quantify exactly how much is earned at each step of the project. It is even conceivable that the project will fail in its later stages of development, resulting in the loss of most or all of the implied profit earned up to that time.

Two points in the development process are of primary importance to the appraiser. Generally the appraiser is asked to estimate the value of the underlying land. The effective date of this value estimate is usually just before the beginning of construction. Since no entrepreneurial profit has been earned at this point, it would not be logical for the appraiser to allow for entrepreneurial profit as well as monetary investment return. The second important date is the prospective date of value, the date when all construction (including signs, landscaping, etc.) has been completed but no lots have been sold. The value estimated under this premise is referred to as the *prospective value of the project upon completion.*

The premise that no lots have been sold at project completion is somewhat artificial since some lots are typically sold before all construction is completed. The appraiser generally does not have data to indicate how much entrepreneurial profit is earned during the development phase. It is unclear, therefore, what level of entrepreneurial profit should be deducted under this premise.

It could be argued that the project might be purchased by a passive investor at the point of completion. The investor would certainly have to deduct sales and overhead expenses before receiving any return on capital, but it would no longer be necessary to pay a developer to oversee the project. In other words, the investor would not have to get involved in project development. In this case it would be assumed that the developer had earned most of his profit when the project was completed. In estimating the wholesale value of this project, the appraiser might not make a separate deduction for entrepreneurial profit, but the discount rate might be increased to reflect the entrepreneurial profit earned during sellout.

On the other hand, it could be argued that a project is not complete until it is sold out. Most recent literature on subdivision analysis tends to take the former rather than the latter approach, assuming that some entrepreneurial profit is earned upon completion of project construction. It seems, however, that the appraiser is in the best position to decide when the bulk of the risk is incurred—during construction or during sellout.

Land Value—Variable Loan Amount   Sometimes the amount of the land loan is a function of the final value estimate. In this case, two unknowns are introduced into the problem, so there is no simple mathematical solution. An answer can be derived with iteration; using the circular reference feature of a spreadsheet computer program; using a formula approach like the Ellwood or Akerson formulas used to estimate the value of other income-producing properties; or using a computer program. A formula approach for estimating land value is demonstrated below.

The first step is to calculate the net cash flows before considering the loan. This is like determining the net operating income of a property held for investment such as an office building. The basic valuation formula is

$$\text{equity value} = (\text{net cash flows} - \text{principal payments} - \text{interest payments}) \times PV$$

This problem is concerned with the land loan only and an 18% equity discount rate is used. (See Table 35.)

Table 35—Net Cash Flows Before Financing

Semiannual period beginning	1/93	7/93	1/94	7/94	1/95	Totals
Source of cash						
Sales income	$ 0	$520,000	$485,000	$461,500	$461,500	$1,928,000
Total cash	$ 0	$520,000	$485,000	$461,500	$461,500	$1,928,000
Use of cash						
Development costs	$550,000	$ 0	$ 0	$ 0	$ 0	$ 550,000
Selling costs	0	62,450	58,250	55,315	55,315	231,330
Admin./overhead	15,500	29,250	24,900	20,850	16,950	107,450
Entrepreneurial profit	55,000	41,600	38,800	36,920	36,920	209,240
Total costs	$620,500	$133,300	$121,950	$113,085	$109,185	$1,098,020
Net cash flow	–$620,500	$386,700	$363,050	$348,415	$352,315	$ 829,980

The following land loan terms are assumed:

Loan-to-value ratio	75%
Interest rate	11% (5.5% per semiannual period)
Repayment terms	125% (loan payments as percentage of unit sales)
Loan amount	$0.75\,V$ (75% of value)

The principal and interest payments required to amortize the loan are shown in Tables 36 and 37. Now the value of the land can be estimated. (See Table 38.)

Thus the implied loan amount is $418,851 (75% of $558,468) and the implied equity value is $139,617. As mentioned previously, this problem could also be solved using iteration, a computer spreadsheet program, or a computer program that incorporates the formulas.

Land Value with a Land Loan and a Site Development Loan

The value of the land can also be found assuming typical financing of both the land and the site development costs. With the addition of the second loan, the risk to the equity position increases and the equity yield rate must be increased from 18% to 20%. The terms of the loan are set forth below.

Land Loan Terms

Loan amount	$400,000
Interest rate	11% (5.5% per semiannual period)
Repayment terms	125% (loan payments as percentage of unit sales)

Note: Interest based on average loan balance

Site Development Loan Terms

Loan amount	100% of site development costs
Interest rate	12% (6% per semiannual period)
Repayment terms	125% (loan payments as percentage of unit sales)

Note: Interest based on average loan balance

Table 39 shows the net cash flows with the site development loan.

▼▼▼

Table 36—Principal Payment Schedule

Semiannual Period	Unit Sales %		Repayment Rate		Loan Amount		Principal Payment
1	0.0	×	1.25000	×	0.75V		0.0
2	0.27273	×	1.25000	×	0.75V	=	0.25568V
3	0.25455	×	1.25000	×	0.75V	=	0.23864V
4	0.23636	×	1.25000	×	0.75V	=	0.22159V
5			0.04545*	×	0.75V	=	0.03409V

*Percentage of loan balance remaining in the fifth period

Table 37—Interest Payment Schedule

Semiannual Period	Average Balance					Interest Amount		Interest Payment
1	(1	−	0	)	×	(0.75V) × (0.055)	=	0.04125V
2	(1.00000	−	0.34091/2)		×	(0.75V) × (0.055)	=	0.03422V
3	(0.65909	−	0.31819/2)		×	(0.75V) × (0.055)	=	0.02062V
4	(0.34090	−	0.29545/2)		×	(0.75V) × (0.055)	=	0.00797V
5			0.04545/2		×	(0.75V) × (0.055)	=	0.00094V

Table 38—Land Value Estimate

Period	Cash Flow		Principal		Interest		PV Factor @ 9%	
1	(−$620,500	−	0	−	0.04125V)	×	(0.91743) =	−$569,265 − 0.03784$V$
2	($386,700	−	0.25568V	−	0.03422V)	×	(0.84168) =	$325,478 − 0.24400$V$
3	($363,050	−	0.23864V	−	0.02062V)	×	(0.77218) =	$280,340 − 0.20020$V$
4	($348,415	−	0.22159V	−	0.00797V)	×	(0.70843) =	$246,828 − 0.16263$V$
5	($352,315	−	0.03409V	−	0.00094V)	×	(0.64993) =	$228,980 − 0.02277$V$

$$0.25V = \$512,361 - 0.66744V$$
$$0.91744V = \$512,361$$
$$V = \$558,468$$

Also shown: $\$512,361 - 0.66744V$

Table 39—Net Cash Flows with Site Development Loan

Semiannual period beginning	1/93	7/93	1/94	7/94	1/95	Totals
Source of cash						
Sales income	$ 0	$520,000	$485,000	$461,500	$461,500	$1,928,000
Development loan proceeds	550,000	0	0	0	0	550,000
Total cash	$550,000	$520,000	$485,000	$461,500	$461,500	$2,478,000
Use of cash						
Development costs	$550,000	$ 0	$ 0	$ 0	$ 0	$ 550,000
Selling costs	0	62,450	58,250	55,315	55,315	231,330
Admin./overhead	15,500	29,250	24,900	20,850	16,950	107,450
Entrepreneurial profit	55,000	41,600	38,800	36,920	36,920	209,240
Interest on land loan	22,000	18,250	11,000	4,250	500	56,000
Principal on land loan	0	136,364	127,273	118,182	18,181	400,000
Interest on development loan	33,000	27,375	16,500	6,375	750	84,000
Principal on development loan	0	187,500	175,000	162,500	25,000	550,000
Total costs	$675,500	$502,789	$451,723	$404,392	$153,616	$2,188,020
Net cash flow	-$125,500	$ 17,211	$ 33,277	$ 57,108	$307,884	$ 289,980
PV of cash flow	-$114,091	$ 14,244	$ 25,002	$39,006	$191,172	$155,333
Value	$555,333					
Annual *IRR*	0.200000					
Equity	$155,333					
Land loan	$400,000					

▼▼

In this case the land loan-to-value ratio is 72.0% ($400,000/$555,333) and the site development loan is $550,000, which is funded gradually over the construction period.

Conclusion In the five applications of the development approach presented, land value ranged from $547,918 to $558,286, a narrow range which approximates the $550,000 value derived using the sales comparison approach. Note that different discount rates were used in the financial analyses to reflect differences in risk, but the values varied only slightly. This is to be expected when the methods are applied correctly.

ESTIMATING PROSPECTIVE VALUE

In addition to estimating land value, an appraiser is typically asked to estimate the prospective value of a proposed subdivision. This is the expected value of the project as of completion, including the construction of all site improvements, but prior to the sale of any of the lots. All value estimates derived using the applicable approaches should reflect prospective values as of this date of completion. This is relatively simple when a single-phase project is being appraised, but a multiphase project may pose problems. When a project is to be built in phases, the prospective value estimate is typically the expected value of the first phase as if it were completed, plus the value of any additional land, plus common site improvements that contribute value to the remaining land. All of these value estimates should be prospective values, reflecting expectations as of the date when the first phase of the project is expected to be completed.

Sales Comparison Approach

As indicated earlier, subdivisions are not usually bought and sold after completion but prior to sellout. There are, however, exceptions in some areas of the country. If sales data on projects sold at completion are available, use of the sales comparison approach would be indicated. To apply this

▼▼▼

approach, the appraiser collects pertinent data from each comparable sale, makes appropriate adjustments for dissimilarities in attributes such as density, location, lot size, project amenities, market conditions, and financing, and ultimately arrives at a value estimate for the project upon completion. Again, this value estimate should be prospective and reflect the expected value as of the anticipated date of project completion.

Cost Approach

To estimate the prospective value of a subdivision with the cost approach, the appraiser estimates the prospective cost of constructing the proposed improvements. All cost estimates should be prospective and reflect expectations as of the anticipated date of project completion. Care should be taken to ensure that the improvements represent the highest and best use of the property. To illustrate the application of the cost approach, the prospective value of the Forest Oaks Subdivision will be estimated as of July 1993. The land value as of January 1993 has already been estimated at approximately $550,000.

Development Cost Estimate   Four steps are involved in preparing a development cost estimate.

1. Preparation of a quantity survey
2. Selection of units of measure
3. Selection of unit costs
4. Selection of cost multipliers

A complete quantity survey of site improvement costs is shown in Table 40. (This information was presented earlier in Table 1.)

Indirect Costs   Next, indirect costs are identified and estimated. In Table 41 they are combined with direct costs and entrepreneurial profit is added as a percentage of site improvement costs. Finally a time adjustment is applied to produce a prospective value estimate by the cost approach.

▼▼▼

Table 40—Site Improvement Costs

Item	Unit	Quantity	Unit Cost	Total
Lot clearing	Acre	9	$3,000.00	$27,000
Grading	Sq. ft.	131,600	0.17	22,372
4-in. rock	Sq. ft.	131,600	0.55	72,380
4-in. asphalt	Sq. ft.	131,600	0.80	105,280
1-ft. concrete curb	Lin. ft.	10,200	6.75	68,850
8-in. sewer main	Lin. ft.	3,400	15.50	52,700
4-in. sewer laterals	Lin. ft.	780	8.55	6,669
Sewer manholes	Each	10	1,225.00	12,250
Storm drains	Lin. ft.	3,400	20.00	68,000
6-in. water lines	Lin. ft.	3,400	13.75	46,750
1-in. water laterals	Lin. ft.	780	3.65	2,847
Underground street lights	Each	19	1,420.00	26,980
Underground electrical	Lin. ft.	4,160	2.45	10,192
Erosion control	Acre	27	300.00	8,100
Subtotal				$530,370
Contingency (10%)				53,037
Subtotal				$583,407
Cost multiplier				x 1.00
Current multiplier				x 0.86
Adjusted subtotal				$501,730
Total site improvement cost			Rounded	$500,000
Plus engineering fees				25,000
Plus indirect development costs				25,000
Total				$550,000

Only a portion of the total entrepreneurial profit to be earned in the project is included in the costs of the project upon completion. The remaining entrepreneurial profit will be earned during the sellout period. In situations in which the approval and construction processes represent the riskiest parts of the development, a larger portion of the entrepreneurial profit may be recognized at the point of completion.

Table 41—Cost Summary

Direct costs	
Land	$ 550,000
Site	500,000
Engineering	25,000
Subtotal - direct costs	$1,075,000
Indirect costs	
Site costs	$ 25,000
Overhead/taxes	15,500
Total costs	$1,115,500
Entrepreneurial profit (10% of site improvement costs)	55,000
Total	$1,170,500
Time adjustment @ 3% (6 months)	35,115
Prospective value estimate by cost approach	$1,205,615

Development Approach

Again, the development approach is applied under different premises. The four applications that follow demonstrate estimation of

1. Prospective value—no financing
2. Prospective value—no deduction for entrepreneurial profit
3. Prospective value with financing
4. Prospective value with project loan as a percentage of value

Prospective Value —No Financing   To estimate the prospective value of a completed subdivision by the development approach, the appraiser prepares a cash flow forecast of all incomes and expenses expected after the project is completed—i.e., the incomes expected to be realized and the expenses expected to be incurred during the sellout period. These net cash flows are then discounted at an appropriate rate to reflect the value of the project upon completion but prior to sellout. As illustrated in the land valuation section, the development approach can be undertaken either with or without considering financing. If the report is to be used as a guide in financing the project, the analysis should assume financing to give the

▼▼▼

lender an idea of how financing will affect the cash flows. Table 42 is a sales and construction schedule for the subdivision project. Sales are forecast to begin in July of 1993.

Table 42—Sales and Construction Schedule

Semiannual period beginning	7/93	1/94	7/94	1/95
Beginning balance	55	40	26	13
Sales				
Cul-de-sac lots	5	5	4	4
Corner lots	3	2	2	2
Interior lots	7	7	7	7
Total sales	15	14	13	13
Ending balance	40	26	13	0
Cumulative sales	15	29	42	55

Tables 43 and 44 show the project's net cash flow forecast and the calculation of present value.

Table 43—Net Cash Flows

Semiannual period beginning	7/93	1/94	7/94	1/95	Totals
Source of cash					
Sales income	$520,000	$485,000	$461,500	$461,500	$1,928,000
Total cash	$520,000	$485,000	$461,500	$461,500	$1,928,000
Use of cash					
Selling costs	$ 62,450	$ 58,250	$ 55,315	$ 55,315	$ 231,330
Admin./overhead	29,250	24,900	20,850	16,950	91,950
Entrepreneurial profit	41,600	38,800	36,920	36,920	154,240
Total costs	$133,300	$121,950	$113,085	$109,185	$ 477,520
Net cash flow	$386,700	$363,050	$348,415	$352,315	$1,450,480

Table 44—Present Value

Semiannual Period	Cash Flow		PV @ 7.5%		Present Value
1	$386,700	×	0.93023	=	$ 359,720
2	$363,050	×	0.86533	=	$ 314,158
3	$348,415	×	0.80496	=	$ 280,460
4	$352,315	×	0.74880	=	$ 263,813
PV of cash flow					$1,218,151
Value	$1,218,151				
Annual IRR	0.1500				

The present value of the project, assuming a 15% annual property discount rate (7.5% per semiannual period) is $1,218,151. The effective date of the prospective value estimate is July 1, 1993, immediately after completion but before the sale of any of the units. The discount period covers four semiannual periods. A line item deduction equal to 8% of sales income was made for entrepreneurial profit.

Prospective Value — No Deduction for Entrepreneurial Profit
Prospective value is calculated in Table 45 without any deduction for entrepreneurial profit. Increasing the property discount rate 10% to 25% (12.5% annually) and eliminating entrepreneurial profit as a line item results in a present value of $1,211,852, which is approximately equal to the $1,218,151 project value estimated with a 15% discount rate and an 8% entrepreneurial profit deduction. In this case the rate of return, or discount rate, represents a return on the invested capital plus a profit to compensate the entrepreneur for the effort expended to create the project and sell all the lots.

Prospective Value with Financing
The prospective value of a subdivision upon completion but prior to sellout can also be estimated assuming financing of the project. The development loan is generally set at a percentage of total project value or at a fixed amount. In this case the loan

Table 45—Net Cash Flows

Semiannual period beginning	7/93	1/94	7/94	1/95	Totals
Source of cash					
Sales income	$520,000	$485,000	$461,500	$461,500	$1,928,000
Total cash	$520,000	$485,000	$461,500	$461,500	$1,928,000
Use of cash					
Selling costs	$ 62,450	$ 58,250	$ 55,315	$ 55,315	$ 231,330
Admin./overhead	29,250	24,900	20,850	16,950	91,950
Total costs	$ 91,700	$ 83,150	$ 76,165	$ 72,265	$ 323,280
Net cash flow	$428,300	$401,850	$385,335	$389,235	$1,604,720
PV of cash flow	$380,711	$317,511	$270,633	$242,997	$1,211,852
Value	$1,211,852				
Annual *IRR*	0.250000				

amount is fixed and interest and principal payments are periodically deducted from cash flows. The applicable discount rate is the equity yield rate.

Table 46 presents a cash flow forecast and value estimate for the property assuming the following loan terms:

Project Loan Terms

Loan amount $950,000

Interest rate   12% (6% per semiannual period)

Repayment terms   125% (loan payments as percentage of unit sales)

Note: Interest based on average loan balance

In Table 46 the equity yield rate is increased to 20% and the value estimate
is $1,243,687, very close to the $1,218,151 value estimate derived using a
15% discount rate without financing. Comparing these scenarios highlights
the impact of financing on the rate of return.

▼▼▼

106

Table 46—Net Cash Flows

Semiannual period beginning	7/93	1/94	7/94	1/95	Totals
Source of cash					
Sales income	$520,000	$485,000	$461,500	$461,500	$1,928,000
Total cash	$520,000	$485,000	$461,500	$461,500	$1,928,000
Use of cash					
Selling costs	$ 62,450	$ 58,250	$ 55,315	$ 55,315	$ 231,330
Admin./overhead	29,250	24,900	20,850	16,950	91,950
Entrepreneurial profit	41,600	38,800	36,920	36,920	154,240
Interest on development loan	47,284	28,500	11,011	1,295	88,090
Principal on development loan	323,864	302,273	280,682	43,181	950,000
Total costs	$504,448	$452,723	$404,778	$153,661	$1,515,610
Net cash flow	$ 15,552	$ 32,277	$ 56,722	$307,839	$ 412,390
PV of cash flow	$ 14,138	$ 26,675	$ 42,616	$210,258	$ 293,687
Value	$1,243,687				
Annual *IRR*	0.20000				
Equity	$ 293,687				
Development loan	$ 950,000				

Prospective Value with Project Loan as a Percentage of Value

The development approach can also be applied to estimate prospective value assuming a development loan based on a percentage of total project value. The following loan terms are assumed:

Project Loan Terms

Loan-to-value ratio	75%
Interest rate	12% (6% per semiannual period)
Repayment terms	125% (loan payments as percentage of unit sales)

Note: Interest based on average loan balance

Table 47 shows the net cash flows from the project, which are used to derive a prospective value estimate.

With the equity yield rate increased to 20%, a value estimate of $1,241,935 is derived, nearly equal to the $1,218,151 value estimate calculated with a 15% discount rate and no financing. Again, the impact of financing on the rate of return is obvious.

A computer program was used to prepare the preceding tables, but an appraiser could also use a formula approach or trial and error to find these answers. Regardless of the method applied, the solutions should be the same if an identical set of assumptions is used.

TWO TESTS OF FEASIBILITY

The feasibility of a project can be tested by comparing the cost of the project upon completion of construction with the present value of the project or by calculating threshold rates of return. Both of these methods are demonstrated.

Table 47—Net Cash Flows

Semiannual period beginning	7/93	1/94	7/94	1/95	Totals
Source of cash					
Sales income	$520,000	$485,000	$461,500	$461,500	$1,928,000
Total cash	$520,000	$485,000	$461,500	$461,500	$1,928,000
Use of cash					
Selling costs	$ 62,450	$ 58,250	$ 55,315	$ 55,315	$ 231,330
Admin./overhead	29,250	24,900	20,850	16,950	91,950
Entrepreneurial profit	41,600	38,800	36,920	36,920	154,240
Interest on development loan	46,361	27,944	10,796	1,270	86,371
Principal on development loan	317,540	296,371	275,202	42,339	931,452
Total costs	$497,201	$446,265	$399,083	$152,794	$1,495,343
Net cash flow	$ 22,799	$ 38,735	$ 62,417	$308,706	$ 432,657
PV of cash flow	$ 20,726	$ 32,012	$ 46,895	$210,850	$ 310,483
Value	$1,241,935				
Annual *IRR*	0.20000				
Equity	$ 310,483				
Development loan	$ 931,452				

Cost of Completion vs. Present Value

A critical point in any project is the time when construction is completed but none of the units have been sold. This is generally the point of greatest financial exposure. To test the feasibility of a project at this point in time, the appraiser compares the value estimate reached in the cost approach with the value estimate produced in the development approach. The value estimates derived for the Forest Oaks Subdivision were estimated as of July 1, 1993, the projected date of completion. The results of both approaches are summarized in Tables 48 and 49.

Table 48—Cost Approach Summary

Direct costs	
Land	$ 550,000
Site improvements	500,000
Engineering fees	25,000
Subtotal	$1,075,000
Indirect costs	$ 25,000
Overhead/taxes	15,500
Total costs	$1,115,500
Management/entrepreneurial profit (10% of site improvement, engineering, and indirect costs)	55,000
Total	$1,170,500
Time adjustment @ 3% (6 months)	35,115
Prospective value estimate	$1,205,615

Table 49—Development Approach Summary

Net Cash Flows

Semiannual period beginning	7/93	1/94	7/94	1/95	Totals
Source of cash					
Sales income	$520,000	$485,000	$461,500	$461,500	$1,928,000
Total cash	$520,000	$485,000	$461,500	$461,500	$1,928,000
Use of cash					
Selling costs	$ 62,450	$ 58,250	$ 55,315	$ 55,315	$ 231,330
Admin./overhead	29,250	24,900	20,850	16,950	91,950
Entrepreneurial profit	41,600	38,800	36,920	36,920	154,240
Total costs	$133,300	$121,950	$113,085	$109,185	$ 477,520
Net cash flow	$386,700	$363,050	$348,415	$352,315	$1,450,480
PV of cash flow	$359,721	$314,159	$280,460	$263,814	$1,218,154
Value	$1,218,154				
Annual *IRR*	0.15000				

111

The value derived using the development approach ($1,218,154) is greater than the value indicated by the cost approach ($1,205,615), which suggests that the project is feasible. To make a fair comparison, the appraiser must be sure that the values are estimated as of the same date and that the same level of completion is assumed in each approach.

Calculating Threshold Rates of Return

A second way to test feasibility is to prepare a set of cash flows covering both the construction period and the sellout period, select an appropriate initial value for the land, and calculate an internal rate of return. If this rate of return is equal to or greater than the expected return on a typical investment, the project is feasible. Table 50 presents a cash flow forecast for the subject subdivision project prepared on an unleveraged basis (without financing). Project cash flows are summarized in Table 51 and internal rates of return are calculated.

If the *IRR* of 15.4% (indicated in Table 51) is equal to or greater than the typical rate of return expected by an investor, the project would be considered feasible.

Table 50—Net Cash Flows

Semiannual period beginning	1/93	7/93	1/94	7/94	1/95	Totals
Source of cash						
Sales income	$ 0	$520,000	$485,000	$461,500	$461,500	$1,928,000
Total cash	$ 0	$520,000	$485,000	$461,500	$461,500	$1,928,000
Use of cash						
Development costs	$550,000	$ 0	$ 0	$ 0	$ 0	$ 550,000
Selling costs	0	62,450	58,250	55,315	55,315	231,330
Admin./overhead	15,500	29,250	24,900	20,850	16,950	107,450
Entrepreneurial profit	55,000	41,600	38,800	36,920	36,920	209,240
Total costs	$620,500	$133,300	$121,950	$113,085	$109,185	$1,098,020
Net cash flow	–$620,500	$386,700	$363,050	$348,415	$352,315	$ 829,980

▼▼▼

113

▼▼

Table 51—Cash Flow Summary

Semiannual Period	Cash Flow
0	−$550,000
1	−$620,500
2	$386,700
3	$363,050
4	$348,415
5	$352,315
IRR = 7.7% semiannually, or 15.4% annually	

INDEX

Page numbers in italic type identify references to material in the Forest Oaks Subdivision Case Study.

115

▼▼▼